Fraud 101

Techniques and Strategies for Understanding Fraud
Third Edition

STEPHEN PEDNEAULT

John Wiley & Sons, Inc.

Published by John Wiley & Sons, Inc., Hoboken, New Jersey.
Published simultaneously in Canada.

For general information on our other products and services, or for technical
support, please contact our Customer Care Department within the United States
at (800) 762-2974, outside the United States at (317) 572-3993, or via fax (317)
572-4002.

Wiley also publishes its books in a variety of electronic formats. Some content
that appears in print may not be available in electronic books. For more
information about Wiley products, visit our web site at www.wiley.com.

Library of Congress Cataloging-in-Publication Data:

Pedneault, Stephen, 1966-
    Fraud 101 : techniques and strategies for understanding fraud / Stephen
    Pedneault.–3rd ed.
        p. cm.
    Includes bibliographical references and index.
    ISBN 978-0-470-48196-7 (cloth)
    1. Commercial crimes–Investigation–United States. 2. Fraud investigation–
United States. I. Title. II. Title: Fraud one hundred one. III. Title: Fraud one
hundred and one.
    HV6769.D38 2009
    363.25'963–dc22   2009015530

Printed in the United States of America

10 9 8 7 6 5 4 3 2 1

For Justin, Evan, and Kim

Contents

Preface

At the time of this writing of the third edition of *Fraud 101*, the U.S. economy is facing extraordinary challenges. Wall Street and the entire global economic and financial system are in steep decline, and the economy is in a worldwide recession. Financial institution Lehman Brothers recently filed for bankruptcy, the insurance giant AIG is in dire financial straits and required taxpayer bailouts to survive, and the mortgage giants Fannie Mae and Freddie Mac are in deep jeopardy. The U.S. federal government approved a historic funding package of up to $750 *billion* in stimulus payments to be made to various financial markets and industries in distress with the goal of stimulating the economy. Payments to date appear to have had little impact with no proven results on the economy.

In one of the most egregious cases in history, Bernard Madoff, a financier and investment manager, recently admitted to embezzling more than $50 *billion* of investors' funds through an elaborate Ponzi scheme he perpetrated. Allegedly, the money he paid to early investors was from funds received from subsequent investors, and when too many investors demanded their funds in response to the failing economy, the scheme collapsed. Although Ponzi schemes are common and have occurred many times in history, Madoff's scheme is the largest Ponzi scheme ever. The dimension of fraud cases is becoming unfathomable—multi-millions and even billions are becoming commonplace.

In one recent case detected in my home state of Connecticut last month, the sole equity partner of a six-office, 238-attorney law firm was accused of stealing more than $350 million in client funds. One person—$350 million. The question that remains is just how many of these schemes exist today and continue to go undetected?

"Identify theft," a buzz word for the past two years, has been replaced by "subprime lending," "mortgage fraud," and record-setting foreclosures. Financial lending has come to a grinding halt, with money no longer moving between institutions, and interest rates have been cut to record lows by the Federal Reserve in the hope of jump-starting the economy. It's not a particularly great time in history from an investor's perspective, but an extremely interesting time for fraud professionals.

It is not unusual for policies and practices to have a direct link to increases in fraudulent activity. To examine identify theft for a moment, we would start by looking back to see how personal and financial information was safeguarded. We would not have to look far into the past to see that Social Security numbers appeared on many items, including insurance cards, voter registration cards (a matter of public record), and class lists posted on every professor's office door in most every college and university. The use of shredders has only become commonplace in most businesses and homes since identity theft became an issue. The earlier practice was to simply throw away old and unwanted information, which allowed thieves to capture critical information merely by going through the garbage. With so much personal and financial information proliferated under past practices, it is no wonder identify theft became such an issue.

The same holds true with the new mortgage fraud industry. Prior to subprime and other questionable lending practices, would-be borrowers were required to substantiate their income and assets and support their applications for loans with credible documentation. The application package was scrutinized and verified, and the borrower would be allowed to borrow only up to a maximum value of the property. Borrowers could only borrow funds up to a limit they could afford to repay monthly, including real estate taxes and insurance costs, and also have some residual funds for living expenses. Loan products offered as late as 2006 and 2007 offered borrowers the ability to purchase homes well beyond their price range, with little to no income verification performed. Borrowers could state their income without providing any support and could borrow up to 100% of the value of the property with no money down. It is no wonder the foreclosure rate has reached historic levels, leading to the discovery of mortgage fraud in many of these deals. Individuals participating in real estate closings were often compensated with a commission for each closing, creating a financial incentive for lenders and mortgage brokers to solicit and close as many purchases and refinances as possible, at any cost. It is only after the mortgage industry's collapse that we are finding out that many real estate professionals, including real estate agents, appraisers, lenders, mortgage brokers, and real estate attorneys fudged documents, inflated values, and perpetrated other intentional acts to ensure closings occurred.

Although it is too recent for reaction, the Madoff investment scandal will no doubt forever have an impact on the investment community and industry. New rules will likely result, and investors will review their accounts and investments in a different light, especially if an outside investment firm is involved. Future investment decisions and the ways those investment decisions are tracked will forever be examined in light of Madoff's scheme, with the goal of ensuring what happened with the funds invested with Madoff never happens again.

According to the Association of Certified Fraud Examiners' 2008 Report to the Nation on Occupational Fraud and Abuse, approximately 7% of an entity's gross revenue is lost to fraud. When the 7% estimate is applied to the Gross Domestic Product, the loss due to fraud approximates $994 billion each year. In reality, the figure is likely even higher, as most frauds go unreported—or worse, have yet to be detected.

When assessing the frequency of fraudulent activity to gauge just how much fraud has been occurring, it is important to remember that only the most egregious fraud cases receive media and legislative attention. In fact, fraud is not limited to large international corporations like WorldCom and Enron. Fraud can and does occur in any size company or organization, large or small, regardless of their for-profit or nonprofit status, and in every industry. The majority of smaller frauds never appear in the media and become public knowledge, partly due to their size and frequently by investigative design.

Fraud is also not limited to financial statements, disclosures, and reports issued to investors and lenders alike. Employees are stealing from companies at alarming rates, and individuals concoct new schemes almost daily to defraud some program or system for their own personal gain.

It is clear that fraud has become a growth industry and not only for the perpetrators. Fighting fraud through education, prevention, detection, investigation training, and ultimately prosecution and punishment offers unprecedented growth opportunities in various career paths and industries. The passage of the Sarbanes-Oxley Act (SOX) alone, enacted to address fraud and the dire need for adequate internal controls and procedures within publicly traded companies, has resulted in a whole new industry in and of itself.

Fraud can be and often is broadly defined, but to really understand fraud, it needs to be contextualized to identify the characteristics and issues unique to each type of fraud. One of the goals in writing this third edition of *Fraud 101* is to provide the reader with a working definition of fraud in the broad sense, followed with as many examples as possible of various types of fraud based on my personal experience as a forensic accountant and fraud professional for more than 20 years. Unlike many fraud professionals who have spent their careers investigating a specific range of fraud schemes, I have been fortunate in having the opportunity to apply my knowledge and experience in fraud prevention and investigation in a wide variety of contexts.

Building on the previous editions of *Fraud 101* by Howard Davia and then Howard Silverstone, this third edition brings to focus two areas of fraud: financial statement fraud and employee fraud, including embezzlement. The new edition also provides an investigative approach and new discussion regarding investigative issues, including alternatives for resolving fraud-related matters. Lastly, as with previous editions, new case studies are included to illustrate various fraud schemes in rich detail.

In updating this book, I recognized that many great books exist detailing the history of fraud, various theories on fraud, fraud motivators, deviant traits and tendencies, prevention recommendations, investigative techniques, and other generalized information. Those books provide the depth and detail needed to become and remain proficient in this specialized field. I own most of them. However, there is also a need for books designed to introduce professionals, as well as non-accountants, to the specialized field of fraud. This book is meant to be a valuable introduction to the subject of fraud for those who have little to moderate experience dealing with it, whether preventing, detecting, or investigating it.

The approach used in this third edition is to explain fraud in a practical, easily understood manner, supplementing discussions with real-world case studies that clearly illustrate the fraud issues and schemes discussed. Three detailed cases based upon actual fraud investigations have been included as Appendices to illustrate examples of how fraud schemes are perpetrated, detected, and investigated. Each case concludes with practical advice on how the fraudulent activity could have been prevented or detected earlier, thus minimizing the loss experienced by each victim organization. Experienced fraud professionals seeking to expand and enhance their well-developed skill set may feel this book is basic, although the cases may enlighten even the most seasoned investigator.

While it would be ideal and efficient to discuss every possible aspect of fraud in every possible context all in one book, it would also be an impossible undertaking. As you will learn, the details of any one specific type of fraud could be expanded and detailed within a book dedicated only to that type of fraud, and many of those books exist today. My hope is that you will find this book a valuable introduction to how fraud works and how to prevent, detect, and prosecute fraud that could be occurring in your organization.

Stephen Pedneault
January 2009

Acknowledgments

To my family, who has both supported and tolerated my undertakings and at times crazy schedule, setting the bar high and expecting nothing less.

To my friends and trusted advisors, who have supported my career decisions, have taken personal interest in my success, and have helped bring to light the things they saw in me.

To Helen Koven, my friend and publicist, who gave me the push I needed to begin to document more than 20 years of experience in fraud and forensic accounting in a way that takes the complex and makes it easily understood by accountants and non-accountants alike.

To the folks at Wiley, who gave me this opportunity to expand into the world of writing, opening new doors into my future.

To Joseph T. Wells, founder of the Association of Certified Fraud Examiners, for his foresight into the need for a specialist cross-trained between accounting and investigations, and for providing me with someone to follow as my role model in becoming a national expert in this specialized field.

And to James Ratley and everyone in the Association of Certified Fraud Examiners down in Austin, Texas, who, unbeknownst to them, have contributed so much towards my success as a fraud examiner.

Introduction

It was a bright sunny day in November. The first frost had set in; leaves were still falling, but most had made it to the ground. I was at my desk when Jim Maxwell called. Jim was a lender at the local branch of a bank just down the street. Jim indicated that one of his customers had called him yesterday to inform him that his company would not be meeting its financial covenants when the company submitted its financial statements at the end of December. Jim indicated that the call came as a surprise to him, as the monthly financial reports the company had been submitting right up through September showed the company performing well and within the covenant ratios. A member of the bank's asset review team had even met with the company's president, Bob Silver, during the summer, and nothing unusual was noted. Jim indicated the bank had a term loan outstanding with Bob's company for $2.5 million, along with a maxed-out revolving line of credit of $1 million.

Jim asked me to schedule a meeting with Bob to review the company's most recent financial reports, and he sent over the company-provided monthly financial statements and reports for my review prior to meeting Bob.

I called Bob and we set a meeting for later in the week. In the meantime, I received the past two years' financial statements and reports, which Bob had provided to the bank. I surveyed the monthly balance sheet and income statement amounts, looking for any anomalies or unusual trends. Nothing significant or unusual noted. I noticed the annual financial statements issued for the past two calendar years had been prepared by a local CPA, a good sign.

I went to the company, and as I waited to meet Bob, I watched a well-dressed man leave the shop area and exit the building through a side door. As he closed the door he glanced back, catching my eye as I watched him leave. Later, I learned he was Bob's CPA.

Bob met me in his conference room and gave me a stack of printed reports. Bob indicated he didn't have much time to spend with me, as he had meetings all day, but said that if I needed anything at all I should ask his business manager, Mary, for whatever I needed.

After a few minutes of general conversation, Bob left for a "meeting," never to be seen again that day. As I flipped through the reports he provided, I noticed right away the reports were merely summarized balance sheets and income statements for October and November, and the most recent bank statement. Not much to spend an entire day examining, and certainly nothing that would identify why the company looked so promising through September, only to have financial issues two months later.

After about ten minutes, I walked around until I found Mary. I introduced myself and asked if Bob could be interrupted to shed light on the financials and answer questions. Mary called someone and was told Bob would not be available. Mary, feeling sorry for me not having what I needed and Bob not being available, asked if there was anything she could do while Bob was tied up. She played right into my plan.

I told Mary that Bob had said she could provide me anything I needed, and asked her if she could generate a detailed general ledger report for the full year, in as much detail as possible. Mary said she had never run a general ledger, but would be willing to run it if she could find it on the report menu. With me leaning over her shoulder, she found the report option on a menu. She generated a complete detailed general ledger for the current year, as well as for the complete prior year. Bingo! This level of detail was what I needed but hadn't been given by Bob.

I thanked Mary and told her there was no need to bother Bob any further. If I had any further questions, she and I could figure them out. I didn't want Mary to tell Bob that she had just provided me all the financial details for both years.

As I opened the report and began flipping through the pages, it was hard not to smile. It felt like finding a puzzle solution that the creator thought was well concealed but was actually sitting in plain view. There were general journal entries, adjustments, posted every month—to sales, costs of sales, and various expense accounts. Then the other side of those entries—fixed asset accounts. Journal entries to fixed asset accounts?

I went back to Mary and showed her how to generate the ledgers with details of every adjustment and journal entry posted in the past two years. More pieces of the puzzle. Mary was unknowingly providing me with the rope I'd use to hang Bob by identifying in detail how her boss had been fooling the bank for at least the past two years. And she was so happy to be learning how to run all these new and wonderful reports she never ran before. Wouldn't Bob be happy with her new skills development?

I spent the day detailing how Bob would record fictitious sales at the end of each month, only to reverse them in the following month. I also found that Bob was identifying expenses in both the cost of goods section and the general and administrative areas, and reclassifying them in total as fixed asset additions. The result of these entries—strong monthly sales, consistent gross margins, and decreasing expenses—led to a stable or improving net profit (bottom line). More good news for the lender was found on the balance sheet side of things: A balance sheet with increased receivables, mostly under 60 days, low accounts payable, and increases to fixed assets (equipment) needed to accommodate the increases in volume. Not a sophisticated scheme, but one that had never been identified because the bank was never provided (or had requested) any details. Bob simply provided the same summarized balance sheet, income statement, and accounts receivable aging month after month.

Toward the end of the day, I once again asked Mary whether Bob could meet with me. Mary indicated that Bob asked me to leave a list of questions and stated that he would review the questions and gather whatever I needed for my review in the morning. I left three questions along with copies of select general ledger pages.

The first thing I asked was for Bob to provide every original vendor invoice for my review for every fixed asset addition in the last two years. The second was for Bob to provide the original sales invoices for all the sales recorded each month via general journal entry. The third and last item I requested was to have the original bank statements available along with the cancelled checks, with the cancelled check supporting each fixed asset addition pulled out for my review. I then left before Bob could emerge and ruin the surprise I had left for him.

The next morning I arrived. There was Bob, pacing, waiting for me in the lobby. We went back to the same conference room, and I asked Bob how he had made out with my list. Bob said he did not have invoices or cancelled checks for the fixed asset additions, as there were no invoices for the additions. I told Bob I knew that when I left last night, but wanted to ask him for them anyway. Bob then went into a diatribe about how he was responsible for 50 employees and their families, and that his entries month after month kept the business open, preserving all 50 positions. Bob said he was never late on any debt or interest payment and that the bank was never harmed by his accounting entries. Rationalization at its best.

The bank brought in a workout team, called some of Bob's debt, and fined Bob through increased interest rates and tighter terms. In the end, the bank retained Bob as a customer, but was committed to keeping a closer eye on him. In my last meeting with Bob, he told me that if he had to do everything all over, he wouldn't do things the same way again.

Six months later, I heard from Jim again. Jim thought I would be interested in a new development involving Bob. Jim's bank auditors visited Bob and obtained general ledger reports (identified by my project). They found Bob was back to adjusting his monthly financial reports again, but this time he was recording fictitious sales with offsets to accounts payable, as well as holding off recording legitimate purchases and expenses until subsequent months. Then I remembered that Bob had told me that if he could go back, he would do things differently. And he had!

Fraud has become a risk for any size organization. However, small businesses continue to be especially vulnerable, as the median loss to employers with less than 100 employees was $200,000 according to the Association of Certified Fraud Examiners' 2008 Report to the Nation. Education is the key to addressing the growing frequency of fraud. The more an organization can learn about fraud in general and the potential fraud risks that threaten the financial stability of the organization's cash flows, the better equipped that organization will be to design and implement measures to prevent fraud schemes from occurring in the first place. In areas where fraud could not be prevented, an organization should implement additional measures to detect fraudulent activity as early as practical. Knowledge of different schemes commonly perpetrated, along with signs and symptoms of each scheme, will increase the likelihood that detection will occur.

This book will serve as a great starting point in providing such knowledge and education, but it shouldn't end here.

More detailed information exists in every area of fraud, building on the information provided in this book. I encourage you to seek out additional books, materials, and articles on fraud, which are easily accessible online, in libraries, and in stores, with the goal of staying abreast of changes in the fraud field. It is only through this commitment to constant education that organizations, employers, and individuals alike will remain well-informed of the latest schemes and fraud issues.

CHAPTER 1

The World of Fraud

I am often asked for my thoughts on fraud. A common question posed is whether I believe fraud is on the rise. My response usually goes like this: "When you say fraud, what do you mean by fraud, and what kind of fraud are you talking about? If you are asking me about fraud in general, my answer is yes, I believe fraud in general has significantly increased during my professional lifetime. If you are asking me if society has become less honest and more accepting of individuals who are trying to beat the system, my answer again would be yes. However, are you referring to a particular area of fraud?"

Definition of Fraud

What is fraud? Although there are common definitions of fraud, no two definitions are the same. If an employee brings home some office supplies for their kids to use with their school projects, is that fraud? Or is it simply an employee stealing office supplies? Or is it just an accepted practice in business that some office supplies may end up being used for personal purposes—a cost of doing business, if you will? Or are we saying the same thing, but three different ways? How about a business that overstates reserve balances on their financial statements, only to use those overstated balances in future periods to "smooth" earnings trends? Is that considered fraud, or is it simply a widely accepted business practice—technically incorrect, but otherwise allowed and accepted? Lastly, how about a family who wants to have their children attend a particular college that they can't afford? In preparing the financial aid forms, they don't report certain bank and investment accounts, and underreport their true earnings so that their child will be eligible for financial aid. Are they committing fraud, or are they simply working the system to gain access to funds available for that specific reason—to assist families with high tuition costs?

Depending on who is asked each of these questions, we may get consistent answers or (more likely) we will get disparity based on each individual's background, values, and beliefs.

Therefore, before we can get into discussions and cases relating to fraud, it would be a good idea to make sure we are all talking about the same thing—fraud. One of the best resources for an objective, defendable definition of fraud is *Black's Law Dictionary*. According to *Black's Law Dictionary*, fraud is defined as "a knowing misrepresentation of the truth or concealment of a material fact to induce another to act to his or her detriment."[1]

As mentioned earlier, to further define and understand fraud, it has to be discussed within a specific context. Fraud can be further broken down into subcategories of fraud, along with various methods used to commit each type of fraud. Unfortunately, fraud has become prevalent within virtually every aspect of our lives, is accepted by many as the status quo, and acts as a constant reminder of the sad state of society in which we live. Personal characteristics that were likely found within individuals living a socially responsible life, things like ethics, morals, and pride, have been replaced by greed, self-promotion, and the "what's in it for me" mentality.

The Many Types of Fraud

Names like WorldCom, Enron, and Arthur Andersen have become more than commonplace in discussions regarding fraud.

2

Their names and others—such as Martha Stewart, who was found guilty of lying to authorities about possible insider trading, and Richard Hatch, a *Survivor* winner who failed to pay the taxes due on his winnings, can and often are used in analogies of what can go wrong. Instances of fraud occur every day and either go undetected or are deemed not worthy of attention. Only cases involving overwhelming amounts of money or some other news-grabbing aspect make the headlines. Traditionally, only one in nine fraud cases ever appears in the media, which means that for every fraud you read or hear about, eight more will never appear in the public eye.

Two main areas of fraud exist in the world of accounting: *management fraud*, commonly known as financial statement fraud, and *employee fraud*, or embezzlement. Many of the notorious frauds of this and past decades fall into one of these two categories. However, many other categories of fraud or fraudulent activity exist. If you watch the news, read the newspaper, or scan news posts on the Internet, you should be able to name a few more categories. How about political malfeasance? These frauds are committed by elected officials who abuse their office or position, usually for some form of personal enrichment. Bribes, gifts, preferential treatment, bid rigging, and kickbacks involving politicians and elected officials have been the target of many investigations and convictions as seen in so many news stories.

Then, of course, there is tax fraud. Tax fraud can be carried out by any business, organization, or individual, at the federal or state level. And for all the types of taxes that are imposed at the local, city, county, state, and federal level, there exists an equal number of tax fraud schemes committed to minimize each type of tax. Based on personal experience, the rate of occurrence of some form of tax fraud, whether a large scheme or simply minor cheating, is present on virtually every tax return filed.

Rounding out the top most widely known fraud categories are crimes committed at the federal level: wire fraud, mail fraud, and bank fraud, to name a few of the most common. Convictions on these types of fraud are generally easy to obtain. A scheme to defraud involving an electronic banking transaction or simply mailing a check or payment is all it would take for a violation. The use of either means, common in so many schemes, can lead to a conviction of a federal law. The only conviction easier to obtain is obstruction of justice. Simply provide any false statement or fact to a federal investigator and you have committed obstruction of justice.

There is a risk for fraud in every type of social program that exists. Unfortunately, the reality of the situation is that every program in existence has a certain level of fraud; due to limited resources available to combat the issue, many individuals successfully defraud the programs. At the local level, for example, many towns offer residents below a set income level assistance with their town tax bills. Typically, a form needs to be completed by each applicant, along with a copy of the most recent tax return. Change the amounts to lower figures, copy the return, and submit it with the form and you will receive assistance. At the state level, complete the forms required for state aid, remain silent about the children's father working, earning a decent amount, and living in the same home, and the household income then falls below the set levels so that rent assistance will be provided by the state.

Case Study 1.1 – Public Aid Goes "Fraud Proof"

In my state, we have a publicly funded social program available to low-income individuals whereby qualifying recipients receive state aid to purchase food and other qualifying provisions. Our food stamp program used to require individuals to apply for assistance, and once qualified, the individuals received food stamps in the mail each month to be used similar to cash for purchasing food.

There were many fraud schemes perpetrated involving the food stamp program. Food stamps were often mailed to recipients on the same day each month, and the theft of recipients' mail became commonplace, as did simply robbing the recipient of his or her food stamps as they redeemed them. Food stamps became a form of currency on the black market, used in exchange for virtually any item and service. Recipients would pay for things never intended to be covered by food stamps, and in turn the individuals who were redeeming food stamps for food purchases were often living well beyond the intended income levels of the program.

There were also individuals who received multiple food stamp allocations each month by applying and qualifying using different names and multiple addresses. Children of qualified individuals were often claimed by several different individuals in their own qualification process, enabling each applicant to receive more food stamps per month than they were entitled to by listing children who were actually someone else's children who were already receiving food stamp benefits.

I remember waiting in the supermarket checkout lines behind individuals purchasing groceries with food stamps. Although the program required recipients to purchase generic labeled items, they were purchasing brand-name labels intermixed with generic items. I also saw alcohol, cigarettes, magazines and many other non-covered items

(*Continued*)

being purchased. In the stores with more sophisticated registers, the non-covered items would be segregated and could not be paid for using food stamps. The clerk would collect food stamps for the covered items and then I would watch as the customer pulled out a large roll of cash to pay for the remaining items. I often wondered how the person could have qualified for food stamps with such a large amount of cash. In less sophisticated stores, though, all the items (even those specifically deemed as non-qualifying items) went through and were purchased with food stamps.

Once I asked a cashier after the customer had left why the non-covered items were allowed to be paid for by food stamps. The clerk told me that the store is reimbursed by the state for the same amount either way, so why should they tell customers what they can and can't buy with the food stamps? That mentality made the store an accessory to defrauding the food stamp program.

A few years ago, the state recognized the extent of the fraud issues, or more likely decided to finally address the issue and developed a new system. I attended a session sponsored by the food stamp program in which the two individuals who designed the new automated system presented the way the new food stamp system would work. The individuals explained that they had developed a debit card system to eliminate fraud within the program.

Each recipient would be issued a card similar to an ATM card that could be used to purchase qualifying food items. Each card would have an account associated with it, and each month the card would be replenished with the individual's qualifying amount. There would be no mailing of coupons, theft of mail, or robbing recipients. One card would be issued to each recipient, eliminating the risk that recipients would trade cards or use the monthly proceeds as trade in other transactions.

The presentation ended with the individuals feeling confident that their new system would eliminate the prior fraud and abuse, allowing the program to become a better steward over the public's funds.

The program wasn't even a month old when I found myself behind a customer using one of the new cards. I remembered the session, and my interest was piqued to see how this new system would work. I watched as the groceries were rung, and items not covered were segregated for the customary separate cash payment. The individual opened her wallet and removed her state card, then swiped it on the credit card terminal used for debit and credit card purchases. Three swipes later the clerk told the customer the balance on the card was insufficient to cover the cost of the groceries. Without blinking an eye, the customer opened her wallet again and removed three similar cards. By the third card swipe, there were sufficient funds to complete her purchase.

So much for the state's new program! And how much did they invest in this new system?

Financial aid programs are generally available at every private school, from pre-school through college, to assist families who qualify based on income limits and other requirements. Once again, the families often complete the forms and provide a "version" of the latest tax return showing lower than actual income. These fraud schemes are perpetrated against every program in existence.

Case Study 1.2 – Creative Approaches to Funding Higher Education

Many programs have an application process that requires supporting information to be provided to corroborate the information provided. Unfortunately, the programs' screening processes are often inadequate or outdated. Home computers and inexpensive software packages have made it relatively easy to create supporting documentation that, unless scrutinized and challenged, can easily meet the requirements for eligibility for the program. Bank statements can be easily scanned and then altered to reflect any desired balances. Tax returns can be run over and over again using packages like TurboTax to produce different results.

One great example of this type of fraud is the application process for college financial aid. In addition to completing the required forms, the applicant must also provide copies of tax returns and bank statements.

In one of my recent cases involving a business owner, I obtained copies of his personal income tax returns for the past three years. I identified that he was married with two children, and he owned a home estimated at a value of $500,000, located in one of the best sections of our state. The taxes on his home alone were in excess of $10,000, and the total of his itemized deductions in the latest year was nearly $20,000.

The total income he reported on their jointly filed tax return was $3,500. I was beyond words. A family of four, living in a $500,000 house in the most expensive section of our state was living on $3,500 per year? Sure!

On the bottom of each page of their tax returns, there was a reference to the daughter's name and Social Security number. I found a similar reference on each page of the returns for all three years. That was when I realized that the copies of the returns he had given me were the copies he had used to obtain financial aid for his daughter, the one whose name was written on each page of her parent's return—a requirement of the financial aid system.

With a little research, I learned that the daughter was attending the most expensive college in our state. By giving her school versions of their tax returns reflecting little to no income, I surmised the daughter was likely attending based on funds received through financial aid.

It turned out the tax returns were prepared by her father on his home computer using TurboTax and this was simply the "version" he generated to support his application for financial aid for his daughter's college education.

Here's my question: How could this very sophisticated school's financial aid process not be able to identify that the returns provided were obviously false and that the reported income was unreasonably low based on the other information in plain view on the same returns?

Let's look at the world of insurance. How many types of insurance fraud can you name? First, there is the fraud committed in the application process to obtain coverage, regardless of the type of coverage. Fraud can be committed in virtually every type of insurance known to exist. Leave the past health issues off the health insurance application, fail to mention that the vehicle will be used primarily for business on the automobile application, or indicate that you will be living in the property when a tenant has already been lined up. Then there are the insurance claim fraud schemes. Staged accidents, torched cars (especially when the amount owed on the vehicle exceeds the car's value), faked injuries, previous undisclosed health conditions, burglaries that never occurred, fires that were set, water damage that was intentional, thefts that never occurred, and inflated inventories supporting a loss claim are just a few scheme areas. The goal is to obtain free money from the insurance company, who supposedly can afford the pay out, especially since high premiums have been paid to the insurance company on time all along—a "return on investment" rationalization.

Case Study 1.3 – How Many Did I Say It Was?

While attending college, I worked in construction, often building or renovating shopping plazas. The money was better than what I could earn anywhere else, and I was learning a trade that I still use to this day.

In my last year on the job, we were renovating a small shopping plaza that included a jewelry store. We knew all the shop owners and employees, as we interacted with them daily while rebuilding their shops. One sunny afternoon, a man ran out of the jewelry store, followed seconds later by the owner. The owner yelled to stop the guy, as he had just stolen a Rolex watch. The owner chased the thief a short distance, but he had disappeared. It happened so fast, that our crew never had time to come down from the staging to assist in the apprehension.

Within minutes, the police were at the plaza and cruising the neighborhoods looking for the thief. As the store owner spoke with police, he knew pretty quickly that the guy had successfully eluded police apprehension. We overheard the shop owner recount the individual's actions in the store.

The owner stated that the individual came into the store and asked to see different watches. Several were taken out and he tried on different ones. Then all of a sudden he grabbed three watches and ran out the store.

Three watches? We all looked at each other. We all heard the owner, as he ran out of the store, yelling the guy had stolen a (one) Rolex watch. Somehow, once he knew the thief was gone and likely was not going to be caught, the single watch became three watches.

Why would the owner change his story for the police from one to three watches? Simple—seize the opportunity to make some money. The owner had insurance for thefts and robberies. If the owner reported to the police that a single watch was stolen, that would be the most the owner could recover. But by changing the quantity to three watches, knowing there was no one else who could support or refute the claim, the owner could be fraudulently reimbursed for the cost of three watches—a profit from the day's events!

Most of us didn't like the owner after that day and were glad we hadn't had time to get off the staging to get involved with the situation. However, one of the guys on our crew thought what the owner did was perfectly acceptable. Of course he was the same guy who was always scamming something and getting things for little to no cost.

Last year, I handled a case involving the "burglary" of a store. The claim alleged that individuals had cut the alarm wires and emptied the store on a stormy night. No inventory records were maintained, and there were no working cameras in the store.

In reviewing their claim and interviewing the owners, I found that there was actually nothing available to show that there was actually inventory in the store to steal that night. The only thing I could show was that wires were in fact cut, but there was no evidence to establish whether the wires were cut by burglars or by the owners themselves. Staged burglaries for insurance claims are all too common.

(Continued)

The claim included a listing of the inventory alleged to be in the store along with the associated costs. No supporting invoices were provided showing how the items had been purchased.

Through interviews with the owners, I learned the quantities were determined based on quantities that were typically maintained of each item, not by the actual counts on hand—i.e., what should have been there versus what was actually there. Better still, the costs were not based on what the owners actually paid for each item. The costs used in their claim were based on an average cost they would pay today to replace the items. Additionally, the owners had no records to show how long their inventory had been on hand.

In the end, the claim was denied for lack of supporting information. Nothing could ever be provided to show that the inventory was actually in the store that night or that the owners hadn't simply removed the inventory from the store and claimed a burglary occurred.

Financial institutions have their share of fraud as well, committed by both banking customers and bank employees alike. Retail banking schemes could include opening new accounts under false pretenses or using fraudulent information, passing stolen or counterfeit cash or checks, and kiting (building up a fictitious balance in an account). The lending side of banking is at risk for loan application fraud, collateral fraud (the collateral is nonexistent, fictitious, or owned by someone else), and financial statement fraud. Mortgage fraud alone has developed into a multifaceted area for fraud investigations, involving attorneys, appraisers, real estate agents, mortgage brokers, loan originators, lenders, and anyone else party to a real estate closing.

Linked to financial institution fraud are investment fraud schemes. Hedge fund managers and investment advisors

churning investments to generate commissions, outright steal-ing investments or proceeds from inactive investment accounts, and issuing fictitious statements to account holders to conceal the activity are all common practices. Certainly, Bernard Mad-off's Ponzi scheme may be the largest in history at $50 billion, but as more facts surface about the scheme, it may have been nothing more than an outright theft of investor funds. Two more similar schemes have recently been discovered in my state alone, each approximating $350 million. It makes you wonder just how many of these exist, waiting to be revealed.

While the recent cases with staggering amounts involved have caught significant attention, making it appear as if these schemes are a new phenomenon, the reality is that invest-ment schemes have been occurring ever since individuals have entrusted others with their funds. The following is a case I worked on early in my career.

Case Study 1.4 – Trust Me, We're Friends

Madelyn was in her mid-70s when a young, fresh face anxious to spend time with her befriended her. Lonely for companionship, Madelyn found herself quickly bond-ing with Jackie, an investment manager in her late 20s who worked for the local branch of a national investment firm. Jackie would call or meet Madelyn almost daily, and call her on the days when they didn't meet. They shared the most intimate of details about their lives; Madelyn even attended Jackie's wedding.

Over time, Madelyn developed a sense of trust in Jackie, shifting more and more of her estate over to Jackie's firm for Jackie to manage. Madelyn stayed with Jackie through two maternity leaves and treated Jackie's two children

(Continued)

as if they were her own grandchildren. Madelyn's children and grandchildren were all grown and living in distant states.

Their relationship continued for more than ten years. During that period, Madelyn moved all of her investments to Jackie to manage and was quite happy with how Jackie handled her portfolio.

As Jackie reached 40, Madelyn knew all about the issues arising in Jackie's marriage; before long, Jackie was divorced. Raising two children, Jackie found it harder and harder to continue maintaining the long and demanding hours at the investment firm and was faced with a difficult decision. Jackie contacted Madelyn to discuss the option of leaving the firm to start her own practice, taking with her the accounts and assets she managed, if her clients would follow her.

Madelyn embraced the decision, and soon thereafter, Jackie established her own investment management company. The decision was easy for Madelyn. Jackie had managed her portfolio for so long, eliminating the details and demands of managing her own accounts and assets. How could she survive without her friend's help?

Month after month for the next few years, Madelyn received the regular monthly package from Jackie, just as she did when Jackie was with the investment firm. No major changes were identified each month.

Since going on her own, the time required by Jackie to manage her practice and care for her two children resulted in less contact with Madelyn. One day, Madelyn called Jackie to check on things. Much to Madelyn's surprise, the automated message indicated Jackie's number was no longer in service. Madelyn hung up and tried again, receiving the same message.

Frantic that something happened to her good friend, frail Madelyn contacted a neighbor to help her determine what was happening with Jackie. The friend reviewed samples of Madelyn's investment reports produced by Jackie and compared them from month to month. Nothing unusual was found in the reported assets and activity.

At Madelyn's urging, the friend drove to Jackie's last known address only to find the house empty. The friend returned and advised Madelyn to contact an attorney to look into what happened to Jackie.

I received the call from the attorney, who suspected right away that Jackie had likely stolen all of Madelyn's funds and fled. The attorney had met with Madelyn and her friend and collected all of her investment reports as far back as possible. He provided me with the boxes of her records.

When Jackie worked for the firm, the monthly reports summarizing Madelyn's holdings and investment activity were generated directly from the investment firm's system, a reliable system used by this very well known and established investment firm. The statements showed shares, costs, gains and losses, and provided assurance to the account holder that the portfolio holdings were in fact being held at the brokerage in the customer's account.

However, shortly after Jackie left the firm and started her own practice, the form and format of the monthly reports changed dramatically. Summaries of the investments, along with color graphs and other illustrative depictions of the assets and activity, were included. Jackie had told Madelyn that the new format would make it easier for her to understand and follow her investment account.

However, nothing directly from the investment brokerage was ever included in the monthly package or received

(Continued)

directly by Madelyn, showing that her assets were in fact still in her account.

Month after month, Madelyn continued to trust Jackie and rely on the new reports provided by Jackie until that dreaded day of the unanswered phone call.

I was able to obtain the actual investment account statements for Madelyn's account for the period from when Jackie left the firm to the most recent month. In comparing Jackie's reports to the actual investments provided by the brokerage firm, I found that the assets and activity were properly summarized and included in the new report format by Jackie for the first few months.

Then, I noticed a stock sale and cash disbursement from Madelyn's account. These two transactions never made it into Jackie's reports for the month. Instead, the activity and balances reported by Jackie were summarized as if the transactions never occurred and that the funds remained in Madelyn's account.

Month after month, I watched as Madelyn's assets were sold off, creating large cash balances that were depleted through checks written out of the account. In the months leading up to Madelyn's phone call, the account was fully liquidated and diverted by Jackie, yet the monthly reports Jackie prepared for Madelyn reported all the assets as if no sales had ever occurred and no checks were ever written.

Madelyn lost everything: the best friend she had had in years, a "daughter" and two "grandchildren" she would never see again, and all of her money—a mere $600,000. It was all gone in a heartbeat. I still remember today how she described that feeling as total emptiness and betrayal beyond words, and although Madelyn passed away several years later, hearing the recent stories of Madoff's victims brings her back to mind.

Jackie's whereabouts were determined when a warrant was issued for her arrest. Jackie had fled the state and was located in the South with her two children. I learned that Madelyn was not her only victim, although she was the only victim I investigated. It turned out that Jackie had made off with most of the funds her clients had "entrusted" to her, clients who had followed her when she left the firm to start her own practice. None of the funds were ever recovered.

Had any of the victims requested that monthly investment statements be mailed directly from the brokerage firm that maintained their account, they would have detected Jackie's scheme in the month of the first sale and check.

The point being made in this chapter is that there are many different types of fraud, more than can ever be covered in one book, let alone one chapter. The focus of the remaining chapters will be on financial fraud schemes perpetrated by employees and organizations. In the next chapter, we discuss why fraud is committed, as well as why the occurrences are increasing at an alarming rate.

Note

1. Garner, Bryan A. (ed.-in-chief), *Black's Law Dictionary* 8th edition (West, a Thomson Business: 2004).

CHAPTER 2

Why Is Fraud Committed?

Just as we had to put fraud into context when we discussed the definition of the word, the same holds true when discussing why fraud is committed. The motivations behind fraud vary by type of fraud, as well as by individual case. In general, the overall theme behind committing fraud is some type of financial gain or incentive, but the specific fraud may or may not involve actually receiving monetary enrichment. For example, a small business seeking to keep off the radar screen of the scrutinizing financial institution funding its operations may fudge transactions and balances a bit to meet the financial covenants of the loan arrangement. The controller simply records a portion of the subsequent January sales early in December to make the year-end results. While the company is not gaining any money from the scheme, its actions, including fooling auditors and committing financial statement fraud, avoid potential penalties imposed by the bank for failing to meet covenants, as well as the real possibility of the bank calling their debt. In the end, the company does gain financially, by avoiding penalties and remaining a customer of the bank. Unfortunately some would simply see these actions as part of what happens all the time in business—no harm, no foul.

A Rationalizing Society

Overall, a shift has occurred within a large segment of society that is tired of seeing big government and big business prevail at the expense of small businesses, individuals, and consumers. Financial institutions, too, have received a bad reputation for offering low interest rates yet charging high fees for all their different services, such as ATM charges. Six-to eight-figure (and larger) bonuses paid to individuals who run and manage large underperforming companies often leave the consuming and investing public with a bad taste in their mouths. The recent actions of AIG's management, which included extravagant dining, lavish retreats, and massive bonus payouts in the wake of receiving government bailout funds, are a prime example. Another example was when the leaders of the auto industry flew in their private jets to Capitol Hill to ask for government assistance. Unfortunately, many of the actions of business leaders and politicians have led to a greater acceptance of looking the other way, cutting corners, and cheating the system. Many high-profile cases of fraud or abuse at local, state, and national levels have resulted in little to no consequence to the person responsible, diminishing the perception or threat of any real consequences if anyone else is caught doing the same thing. If given the right opportunity, more people today would be willing to commit fraud and could rationalize their behavior if they were caught. Acting ethically, which historically entailed a single set of standards for defining how one should act appropriately in any situation, has devolved into today's mind-set of *situational ethics*, in which the most appropriate way to act depends on each specific situation. It is an oxymoron, yet more and more people follow this way of thinking, especially if they believe that no one will get hurt and that there will be no consequences if they are caught.

Look at speeding as an example. The posted speed limit on most highways in the United States is 65 miles per hour. If you polled any driving audience and asked by show of hands how many consider themselves speeders, few hands would be raised. If you further defined speeding as exceeding the posted speed limit for any reason, most every hand would go up. Why the change in their response? The most common explanation is that they don't consider themselves speeding if they are only going 10 to 15 miles over the limit, the range set by most police doing radar. In many cases, they may also state they were simply following the traffic. These are two great examples of rationalization for breaking motor vehicle laws. Now change the question and ask the drivers how many of them would follow the posted speed limit if it were absolutely certain that the police radars were set at that limit. All hands would be raised. Why? Because the perceived consequence of being ticketed for speeding is then absolute and would be feared.

For any drivers who claimed to always follow the speed limits, ask them if there were ever a time, driving on any road, under any circumstance, that they had to drive faster or perhaps rolled through a stop sign when they should have come to a complete stop. Not one person could honestly claim to have followed every law 100% of the time. Why? Because each and every driver on the road encounters a time when he or she is either late or in a hurry, and in response has driven too fast, rolled through a stop sign, driven through on a yellow light, and done whatever else it took to make up the time. In most cases, they were never caught, there was no accident, and so there was no consequence to their actions. But it only takes one case to make headlines, and the end results of those "situational ethics" decisions can be catastrophic.

The same holds true with fraud. Fraud occurs every day in many different contexts, and most of the perpetrators are not caught that day. Some will limit their fraudulent behavior to a single act and never be detected; others will continue acting fraudulently each and every day unless, or until, their scheme is revealed. If the fraudster is caught, they may be condemned or cheered, depending on who committed the fraud, who the victim was, and how much was involved.

Financial Statement Fraud

Most of us know of the well-known financial statement frauds committed by publicly traded companies whose stock prices are linked directly to their performance. Huge frauds involving companies such as Enron, WorldCom, Tyco, American International Group (AIG), and Adelphia have had an immeasurable impact on investors and the entire financial market. When the stock price is linked not only to performance but also to executive compensation, via incentive stock options and other financial perks directly tied to the company's stock performance, the motivations become much different. Common schemes include recognizing revenue prematurely, capitalizing operating costs, failing to record or disclose liabilities, related party transactions, special interest entities, fictitious inventory, and inappropriately recognizing costs. The incentive to commit financial statement fraud may be based on promoting the company's overall performance and value as a whole, or it may be based on a single member of management, a stock option holder for example, seeking to maximize personal gain upon redeeming his or her stock options. In either case, the end result is typically a catastrophic decrease in the company's stock price.

It is important, when discussing the motivators for committing financial statement fraud, that one examines each organization on a case-by-case basis. The motivations for a publicly traded company will be different from those of a small, closely held business, and different again from those of a nonprofit organization.

Financial Fraud Comes in Different Shapes and Sizes

Closely held businesses typically have financing in place, which is almost always the reason that the company requires financial statements in the first place, and the debt may include personal guarantees. A personal guarantee means one or more of the business owners personally guaranteed the company's debt to the bank, collateralized with their personal assets. The personal guarantees may be one of the strongest incentives for an owner to commit financial statement fraud—the owner wishes to keep the bank from taking his or her personal residence and investments to repay the debt. How hard would it be for a small company to manipulate its financial results to fool its auditors and the bank?

Case Study 2.1 – Operation MOTT (Move Inventory To Trailers)

A distributor of computer components experienced slower sales than expected. Inventory in the form of computers, laptops, monitors, and ancillary products was ordered in anticipation of a heavy-volume holiday season, filling the warehouses to capacity. Unfortunately, consumer spending decreased that season, and the orders received were much lower than projected. The result was a warehouse full of excess computers heading toward year-end, underachieved sales performance, and severely strained cash flows. The company's line of credit had been nearly tapped to fund the inventory. As the owners strategized to reach a solution, it became painfully clear that the auditors who were coming to observe the year-end physical inventory would readily recognize the unusually high level of inventory in the

(Continued)

warehouse, as well as identify the company's failure to meet bank covenants.

The owners came up with a plan to reduce the inventory on hand in the warehouse. They rented trailers and moved the inventory out of the warehouse into the trailers. One of the owners had a great relationship with an owner of the business across the street, who agreed to allow the company to park several trailers in the unused section of their parking lot at the rear of their building. The trailers were moved across the street and instantly the warehouse resembled what the owners had envisioned when planning sales for the year. To complete the scheme, the owners identified a customer who had placed orders during the year. The demographic information of the customer was changed to a fictitious name and address that the owners controlled. The owners then created real invoices and bills of lading for the sales, keeping the order levels consistent with real orders placed by the customer earlier in the year. Using the owners' personal funds, a few smaller deposits were made into the company's bank account, each one reflected as a payment from the customer against their receivable balance. The cost of the trailer rentals was paid outside of the business.

When the auditors arrived at year-end, the warehouse physical inventory was underway, and the results of their inventory were matched to the perpetual records. During the subsequent audit, sales transactions were traced to original sales invoices and bills of lading and confirmations were sent to the customer to verify the sales terms and outstanding amounts. Since the owners controlled the fictitious customer address, the owners verified and signed the confirmation, then mailed it to the auditors. Even subsequent collections on this customer's receivables could be verified to some deposits received into the company's account.

The auditors completed their fieldwork, issued their financial statements, and were never the wiser that nearly half a million dollars in inventory was simply sitting in unmarked trailers directly across the street.

Motivators Differ by Type of Business

Different types of business have different motivations for fraud. Nonprofit organizations, for example, operate much differently from for-profit companies. Most of these organizations receive some form of funding either at the federal or state level, and many grants or programs require the organization to account for the use of funds received. It is also common for the funding to include requirements that the funds be used only for costs and expenses directly related to the services provided and a provision for the return of any excess funds received but not spent by the end of the grant period. Within this environment lies a whole host of incentives to commit financial reporting fraud.

The first incentive relates to any *give-back* requirements. Obtaining funding, regardless of the nature of the nonprofit organization, has become extremely strained and challenging. All nonprofits have been competing for a larger portion of a diminishing pool of available funds for the past decade. After working so hard to obtain funding, no organization wants to return any portion of the money they actually receive. This may explain why so many organizations whose fiscal year-end is June 30 go on a shopping spree for furniture, computer equipment, and supplies toward the end of May and June. By May, the organizations have determined that they have excess funds that must be spent before year-end to avoid having to return unspent funds. This approach is not a problem if the grants allow for these expenses and they are made prior to June 30. The issues arise when the expenses are not allowed, or if they are made in July or later.

Case Study 2.2 – Accelerated Cost Recognition

An organization received funding from three primary sources that included both federal and state money. Two months before its year-end, the organization determined that all of the funds received during the grant period would not be used, and it was facing the potential to return excess funds. During those last two months, the organization spent funds on what its management thought were legitimate and allowable items; regardless of their valiant effort, however, surplus funds remained at the end of the fiscal year. Determined not to return any of their hard-earned funding, they sought out additional means to spend the funds or at least to report the funds as being spent by the end of the period. The organization looked to the anticipated costs of the new fiscal year. Certain expenses, such as payroll and benefits, would be incurred regardless of the funding in place. To show that the funds were entirely spent with no residual remaining, the organization increased its end-of-year payroll accruals to include anticipated labor costs for the subsequent two months. As of June 30, the accrued payroll amount reported included not only the last week of June's payroll actually paid in July, a legitimate accrual, but also the organization's payroll costs for all of July and August as well.

The organization would have been successful in perpetrating this scheme if its auditor did not perform a comparison of the accrued payroll amount as of June with the prior year's accrued payroll amount. Once the details were provided, the organization was forced to reverse their entries, reducing the accrual and revealing that the funds had not been fully expended within the grant period. The actions of the organization's leadership led the auditor to perform more detailed procedures. In addition to having to refund money to the grantor agency, the organization learned that some of the items purchased in haste during May and June to spend down the funds were determined by the auditor to be unallowable costs under the grant, increasing the amount that had to be refunded.

Employee Schemes

While a portion of financial statement fraud schemes directly benefit the individual perpetrator on a personal level, the individual responsible for committing an employee scheme almost always personally benefits from the scheme. The primary motivator for almost every type of employee scheme is personal financial enrichment of one kind or another. The same holds true with most instances of political corruption and other types of scandals.

What leads an employee to steal customer payments, charge personal items on the company's credit cards, receive vendor kickbacks, or inflate travel expenses is subjective and dependent on the individual's lifestyle. In some cases, the perpetrator has some type of personal financial need, which could include anything from supporting a drug or gambling habit to paying for higher education and medical expenses for a family member. Other cases may be based on the individual's need to fuel a lavish lifestyle, acquiring extravagant assets like houses and cars, taking expensive vacations, and living well beyond his or her means. Some employees steal out of a sense of entitlement, feeling underpaid and underappreciated, while others simply follow the bad example established by the actions of a manager or owner.

Employee theft and embezzlement are not specific to gender or race, and can occur at any position within the organization where opportunity presents itself. Volunteers who collect donations at a charity event have as much access to funds to divert for their personal benefit as do accounts payable clerks who process payments to suppliers and vendors. The more financial responsibilities an individual has within their position, the higher the level of opportunity available to them. The longer an employee has been with an organization, the higher the chances that the employee has established a position of trust over one or more areas of responsibility. Through downsizing and attrition, properly segregated positions are combined into single positions, creating even more opportunity to steal funds and conceal the thefts.

Case Study 2.3 – Unauthorized Cash Discounts

A local business included a retail home remodeling store as well as custom installation services for kitchens and baths. The store's manager was a single mother of three, and her responsibilities included scheduling, coordinating, billing, and collecting for the remodeling projects. The manager's boyfriend was the primary installer, and he managed subcontractors to perform the actual work.

The store's typical customer was a homeowner or contractor, and most sales were paid for by credit card. Refund procedures required the completion of a form along with the manager's signature for approval, and the form was held in the register to be included in the balancing of the drawer at the end of each business day.

One Saturday morning, the bookkeeper met the owner in his office. She was concerned about a sale made at the end of the prior night. A customer came into the store at closing time and purchased paint with the help of the store manager. The customer paid cash, but when the register drawer was balanced in the morning, there was no cash from the previous night's sale.

The owner and bookkeeper began reviewing the night's sales activity and noted a credit card refund processed for the same amount after closing time. There was no supporting refund form in the drawer, and no other customers had come into the store after the paint customer. The bookkeeper highlighted the credit card number associated with the refund processed and retrieved the merchant credit card statements for the previous month. In scanning the statement, they identified and highlighted three refunds. Two of the earlier refunds had been posted to the same credit card number as the one from the prior night. Three refunds were found made to the same credit card in a month, the most recent for the same amount as the cash sale.

Suspecting something was wrong, the owner and bookkeeper retrieved all the merchant credit card statements from the files. Each refund transaction was highlighted and compared; in total, 27 refunds had been processed to the same card number. The owner called the credit card company, and after a significant amount of effort on the owner's part to convince the card company to provide the name on the card, he learned that the card belonged to the store manager.

Meanwhile, the bookkeeper searched for the required refund forms for each transaction, but found none existed. She also reviewed the register details for the days in question and found that cash sales appeared to be heavier on the days

(Continued)

of the refund transactions. The individual dollar amounts of the refund transactions totaled nearly $38,000.

The owner and bookkeeper quickly surmised that the store manager was stealing customer cash sales proceeds on days with significant cash sales and concealing the thefts through fictitious credit card refunds to her personal credit card. It was then they realized that the loss was really $76,000, as the refunds reduced the store manager's outstanding credit card balance at the cost of reducing the credit card proceeds deposited into the company's account.

On Monday morning the owner, armed with advice from counsel, confronted the store manager and placed her on paid administrative leave. When word reached the boyfriend, he was enraged and came to the store to learn more about what had transpired. After hearing the facts, he left for a while. Later that day, he returned and told the owner he would find a way to make restitution to cover the losses.

Concerned about the customer projects in process with no store manager to oversee their completion and collect all remaining payments, the owner identified all the ongoing projects and made a personal visit to each location. On the fifth visit, the customer spoke to the owner and asked him what kind of business he was running. Confused, the owner asked him what he meant by his question. The customer said the boyfriend had offered him a 10% discount if he would pay him directly in cash rather than writing a check to the business.

The owner was furious. The boyfriend had never been placed in a position to negotiate terms with a customer other than through the store at typical payment terms; he was clearly never authorized to collect customer payments in cash at a discounted rate. The owner, concerned that the boyfriend had diverted customer payments from the business, located the boyfriend at another job site, confronted him, and fired him on the spot. The boyfriend told the owner that without his job, he would have no means to make restitution for the amount stolen by the store manager.

When the owner returned to the store, he worked with his staff, using the company's computer system to identify how much was due on each job in process. As they tried to run detailed reports for each contract, they found all the transactions were a mess. Manual files were maintained for each customer and job, but when they looked for a folder for each job in process, no folders could be located. In the older files that were found, they saw inappropriate transactions posted to each customer. A copy of a payment from one customer was in the file of a separate customer project. Change orders to one file were in a completely different customer's folder.

After days and days of sorting the files and computer system reports, the only thing the owner could show was that for the files located, many customer payments had never made their way into the business's bank account. In the end, he was only able to positively confirm that approximately $30,000 in renovation payments had been diverted. However, close to 100 projects had been completed during the time in question, and he was never able to determine the full extent of his loss.

Beyond the stolen funds, which nearly closed his business, the owner lost his store manager of several years and his primary installer—two critical positions for the company, both of which proved difficult to fill with new hires.

The owner lacked employee dishonesty coverage and was unable to recover the stolen funds through an insurance claim. The store manager was arrested and ordered

(Continued)

to pay restitution; she received probation. She never made payments beyond the first two monthly amounts, and skipped the remaining payments. The owner learned that she owned no real estate, was renting an apartment, was behind on her bills, and had no source of income; he decided that pursuing her civilly would generate nothing but more professional fees. He also learned that she had likely stolen the funds to provide a better lifestyle for her three kids—things like televisions and video games in each of their rooms. Her boyfriend was never pursued, as no evidence could link him directly to the diverted funds beyond one customer's statement about his cash payment offer.

In the End

Regardless of the reason why the individual perpetrates the fraud, the end result is usually the same. The employer suffers a financial loss, often involving a significant amount of money, that may or may not be recovered. In addition, professional fees are incurred to investigate and resolve the theft. The organization loses an employee, frequently a key person who performed critical functions, and now must find, hire, and train a replacement. In addition, employee morale is negatively impacted, reducing employee productivity. The whole process results in lost efficiencies, adding to the costs incurred by the employer.

CHAPTER 3

Financial Statement Fraud Schemes

Regardless of the size and nature of an organization, the underlying objective behind every financial statement fraud scheme is to intentionally deceive the users of the financial information being provided. It is important not to limit your concept of fraudulent reporting to audited financial statements. The risk for fraudulent reporting also exists with lower level review and compiled financial statements. However, the level of risk and the number of users of these levels of financials tend to be more controlled.

Before we discuss financial statement fraud, we should understand, in general terms, the process of preparing and issuing financial statements. While the level of scrutiny and procedures performed will be highest with audits, the overall process of issuing financial statements in an audit will be similar to those issued within reviews and compilations. Management is responsible for preparing the financial statements, footnote disclosures, and all aspects of the financial reporting. The organization's internal controls and procedures over financial reporting should include measures to ensure the completeness and accuracy of the financial reports prior to making them available to any parties.

Next, the organization's auditors or outside accountants, if a review or compilation is required, are provided with a copy of the drafted financial statements. The auditors then perform detailed procedures to ensure the organization's financial statements are reasonably prepared in accordance with all professional standards and are free of any material misstatements that could cause the financial statements to be misleading. Procedures performed include independent verification of the amounts and details, recalculations, and other objective measures to corroborate management's balances, results, and disclosures. For the auditors to accomplish their procedures, they must interact with the organization's management and personnel and rely upon information provided to them by the same individuals. Once all the procedures have been performed, the auditors issue the organization's financial statements, along with their opinion. The final or issued financial statements are then disclosed to any required third-party users, such as investors and financial institutions, the two largest groups of financial statement users.

Where Do Things Go Wrong?

Whether issuing an audited, reviewed, or compiled level of financial statements, much of the information provided to the auditors or accountants originates with management. Procedures are performed in an audit to independently corroborate through third parties the information provided by management, such as confirming details with suppliers and vendors, but no such procedures are required for reviews and compilations. Because management controls the information, they can control how much or little is provided to the auditors. When auditors request supporting details—documents such as sales invoices, purchase orders, and time records—these details are provided by management. Depending on the auditor's or accountant's level of training, experience, and skepticism, the documents provided by management may or may not receive much scrutiny.

Herein lays the issue. If the organization's management needs to fool the auditor or accountant into issuing the organization's financial statements with gross inaccuracies or omitting significant details, management controls all the means to make that happen. If, for example, management decided not to disclose certain facts and details, it's likely the auditors would have no other means of knowing that information had been intentionally withheld. Conversely, if management wanted to show results that were different from those that actually occurred, they could fabricate the supporting documents, and the fictitious information and details provided to the auditors would likely pass their scrutiny.

Turnover in public accounting also contributes to the fraud risk issue, as does the diminishing number of individuals who pursue accounting as a career choice. Recruiting for new accountants has become extremely competitive in recent years, and the decline in new accountants has strained many firms' ability to service their clients. Many firms have resorted to having new staff members and college interns perform audit procedures, especially inventory observations. Moreover, if senior accountants are spread too thin over multiple engagements, they may never have the time to make trips out to their clients' sites to oversee and guide their young and inexperienced staff.

Many public accounting firms have grown beyond their capacities, and industry continues to lure the most experienced auditors away from public auditing with better hours and higher compensation potentials. It is not the young auditor's fault for missing fraud during an audit—nothing replaces experience. Although most firms have increased training for new and less experienced auditors, the quality of training may not have reached the level needed to truly combat fraud.

Case Study 3.1 – Engine Light Is On

While working in public accounting, I was responsible for designing audit procedures in response to fraud risks. Based on my experience with the latest developments and trends within the forensic department, I would help determine whether the firm was performing the most practical audit procedures possible. In some cases, the procedures were performed across the board for all audits completed by the firm, while others were performed on a client-by-client basis.

In one particular period, I remember the firm had a series of clients who experienced employee embezzlements perpetrated through cash disbursement schemes. In all of the cases, the client had not realized the scheme was occurring until late in the game, when the amounts involved had grown to significant levels. In each instance, the client had grown complacent with the bank reconciliation process, allowing the perpetrators simply to write checks to themselves knowing their fraud would likely never be detected.

In response to the frauds, the firm looked to me to decide what additional procedures should be added to audits to ensure a cash disbursement scheme would not go undetected, especially one where the checks were payable to the individual directly.

Since the very first audit I was involved in, right out of college, I had always selected monthly bank statements at random during the period to be reviewed. I would ensure all the cancelled checks listed on the statement had been provided, and I would review the statement as well as flip through the cancelled checks, examining the front and back of each check. It was through this simple procedure that I discovered many issues within clients' accounts.

I strongly suggested the firm adopt my procedure and require every auditor to review a sample of monthly bank statements for what I called "reasonableness." The firm agreed with my assessment, and the review of monthly bank statements on a sample basis throughout the audit period was added to every audit program. However, the firm never properly trained the staff, something that became painfully obvious during the heavy audit season.

I met with many audit teams and asked them how the new procedure was working for their client assignments. Each team told me the same thing—the procedure was very straightforward and took little time to complete. None of the teams had identified anything unusual during their reviews.

Then I asked each team to describe their review process, starting with their understanding of the client's cash disbursement approval and check-signing policies and procedures. I got blank looks, like deer in the headlights. Not one team could answer simple questions, such as how many signatures were required on checks and whether there were dual signature requirements.

The analogy I used to explain the problem to the partners was one involving the check engine light in most cars. You are driving down the street and the check engine light goes on, along with some steam coming from the front of the car. You likely pull over and stop the car, then open the hood to see where the issue could be. Once the hood is open, you stare at the engine as if the problem will be painfully obvious, or better yet, as if the problem could be resolved by simply opening the hood. Given the level of electronics and sophistication of most cars today, aside from identifying that the engine was still in fact in the car, few individuals

(Continued)

would have any idea what they were looking at under the hood. Yet we all open the hood and look.

In response, a training session was provided that educated all of the auditors on what information they should obtain and understand in order to form their own expectations regarding the check and disbursement process, prior to reviewing the bank statements and cancelled checks.

Without proper and relevant training and experience, firms will continue to run the risk that their auditors will complete the audit procedures on their engagements without ever truly understanding what it is they are performing and how it relates to the overall financial statements of the client.

Worse still is the declining economy, in which clients are looking for ways to save money and cut costs. Companies are closing their doors, filing bankruptcy, and merging into other entities, all with negative revenue consequences for the public accounting firms' financial situation. In response, auditing firms are placing more and more emphasis on their staff to perform "efficient" audit procedures. Historically, accountants were promoted in large part based on their performance on their engagements, measured most frequently by the profitability to the firm of each client assignment. More pressure exists today to ensure that the engagements remain profitable to the firm.

Given the relatively low experience level of many auditors, the lack of experienced supervision in the field, and the pressure to complete audit procedures within the allotted timeframe per the engagement budget, it is likely that an organization seeking to commit fraud will be able to successfully conceal it from audit detection if the size of the fraud scheme remains under control. Even with better training and a few years of experience, auditors often are no match for the experienced and sophisticated controllers and chief financial officers.

Unfortunately, individuals in the accounting profession are not immune from compromising their professional responsibilities and obligations to protect the public from these schemes. Firms have looked the other way when clients presented false or misleading financial information, either to preserve the client relationship or to receive some form of financial gain (and likely both), undermining their role and the integrity of the entire process. In some instances, auditors or outside accountants have assisted the client in perpetrating financial statement fraud. In others, the organization's accountant has a great relationship with the user of the financial statements, such as a financial institution, where the user may tend to rely on their relationship with the accountant and apply a lower level of scrutiny over the organization's provided financial statements. If the organization's financial performance continues to be successful and the organization provides its financial information in a timely fashion and meets its obligations, the user may never be the wiser. It is only cases in which situations change and the organization experiences a decline or some other event that the past financial statements come into the discussions.

Case Study 3.2 – How Much Inventory Is Too Much?

The bank was getting nervous. One of their manufacturing customers, which had been a great customer of the bank for the past several years, was falling farther and farther behind in its debt repayments. The last set of financial statements provided was of the review level and were issued by a local certified public accounting firm. While the bank was nervous about their $4.5 million line of credit and term debt outstanding, they were somewhat appeased that the

(Continued)

company reported their inventory at $10 million as of December, just three short months ago. The balance sheet appropriately included a reserve for obsolete and slow-moving inventory of $20,000.

On the first visit to the customer's facility, however, it was obvious there was more inventory on hand than they would ever need for their business. Machines were running, producing yet even more inventory, and walking room within the three warehouses was constricted to single-file aisles. Product was stored as high as the ceilings, and more was being produced, with three shifts in operation.

Management's explanation for the overage of inventory was that there were three primary customers for their products, and each required their own unique packaging. They also stated that each customer demanded that its products be ready to ship at a moment's notice, but would not take title to any product until an order was placed and the items physically left the warehouses. The result was an excess inventory of identical products, stockpiled in three different areas depending on the customer and its packaging. To make the situation even worse, management indicated that product sales were decreasing because recently, similar products had begun being imported from the Middle East, selling at a fraction of the company's cost to make the same items.

Upon review of the financial statements issued three months earlier, the bank's auditors revisited the reserve amount reported for slow-moving and obsolete inventory. Next they extracted all the product items from the customer's inventory system, including the last purchase date and last sale date for each item. Focusing only on items that had no purchases or sales activity in the last 24 months, the auditors extracted the current inventory levels and costs associated with any items that had no activity in the past 24 months.

The results were staggering. Notwithstanding the unknown financial impact of the increased competition from foreign competing items, the bank's auditors determined, based on the company's past sales trends, that the true reserve for slow-moving and excess inventory was between $3 and $4 million. Worse yet, the customer was still actively producing more products every hour of every day.

The bank auditors turned their attention to the outside accounting firm and the review that firm had performed. Although an audit had not been performed, meaning that a lower level of scrutiny and procedures had been provided, the bank auditors questioned how the outside accounting firm's reserve calculation of $20,000 just three months earlier could be so far off from the bank auditor's calculated range of $3 or $4 million? It became obvious the customer's balance sheet was grossly overstated and that the bank could easily suffer a loss, as the inventory, if liquidated by the bank to cover their outstanding debts, would only yield a fraction of the costs the customer had incurred to make it.

How could this happen? Quite simply, the reserve calculations and supporting details provided by management were less than complete. Either the accountants did not ask for the right information, they were not provided the best evidence available to make their own determination of the reserve amount, or they fell into the trap of relying too heavily on the client's information, representations, and calculations. In the case study of the bank's manufacturing customer, the owner simply told the accountants that the information they requested to perform an independent calculation of the reserve could not be provided, due to the age and other limitations of the inventory system used. The accountants never pursued the issue, and unfortunately for them management's story proved not to be the case.

When pushed by the auditors, the owner was able to generate the inventory report and export it into Excel for analysis. To determine the activity for identified items within the previous 24 months, the auditors sat in front of computer terminals and manually researched the information on the screens.

The December 2008 report issued by Deloitte's Forensic Center, entitled *Ten Things about Financial Statement Fraud— Second Edition*, identified the financial statement fraud schemes most commonly committed by publicly traded companies, along with frequency of occurrence. Here are the most commonly reported schemes, along with their reported frequencies:[1]

- Improper revenue recognition   38%
- Improper disclosures   11%
- Manipulation of expenses   11%
- Manipulation of liabilities   8%
- Manipulation of assets   8%
- Manipulation of reserves   7%
- Manipulation of accounts receivable   4%

Trend Analysis

Trend analysis is one of the most common means of detecting fraudulent issues within financial statements. Comparing balances and results on the most recent balance sheet, income statement, and statement of cash flows to the same information for prior periods is a common auditing procedure. The ending balances of one year are usually compared to balances for the same period a year ago, such as when current month- and year-to-date amounts are compared to prior year amounts. However, if account balances and results are manipulated each year, these trend analyses may never reveal a potential fraud scheme.

If the trending is expanded to include a comparison of the major account balances for each month in the fiscal year, along with the subsequent months since year end, the analysis may show unexpected results and balances in the months ending each quarter or in the last month of the year, followed by decreased activity in the month immediately following the period end. This may be a sign that the results were manipulated to meet period goals or objectives and were reversed in the subsequent month. The month-to-month trending, especially if performed for the current and past fiscal years, will show if any patterns exist to be further analyzed.

Comparing amounts on the balance sheet or income statement across periods is known as a *horizontal trend analysis*. While many individuals who are contemplating or committing fraud know that auditors will compare annual or quarterly amounts and results, few expect the auditors to use monthly amounts in their trending. Monthly trend analysis of the balance sheet and income statement for a two-year period was standard on all my financial statement engagements.

Another important trend analysis to be performed, especially for the income statement, is a *vertical trend analysis*, in which all the major expense items are shown as a percentage of sales. Once again, the current period's vertical analysis should be compared to prior period percentages, and any significant changes should be investigated and corroborated.

An example of vertical trend analysis commonly calculated is cost of sales and gross margin. Both are shown as a percentage of sales. However, a client who is contemplating committing financial statement fraud, otherwise known as "cooking the books," likely knows the line items and percentages that will be analyzed by their auditors. Therefore, the balances and percentages will be intentionally held to consistent levels from prior periods to avoid additional scrutiny, and the remaining fraudulent transactions will be concealed to other accounts within the income statement and balance sheet. Applying vertical trend analysis to the entire income statement and selected balance sheet accounts may reveal this concealment scheme.

A third trend analysis is to compare related accounts and balances to ensure relationships between the accounts are reasonable. For example, there should be a direct relationship between purchases, sales, and inventory. If sales have increased during the fiscal year and purchases have remained flat compared to the prior year, then inventory should have decreased, as the increased sales had to get the additional items sold from somewhere. The relationships will either be present or not. Auditors need to identify the different accounts that have direct relationships and ensure that, based on the actual results reported, each related account balance reflected the auditor's expected results.

Many organizations and companies have sophisticated accounting and finance departments, commonly staffed by individuals experienced in auditing. Based on past audit experience, the client's accounting staff is often very aware of the audit procedures to be performed and the financial areas the auditors will target. They are also aware of the dollar thresholds auditors often set, known as *materiality*, to determine what balances and transactions will be analyzed. To combat the risk that a client could fool the auditors, the accounting profession's pronouncements strongly suggest that auditors perform more unannounced procedures and add procedures not expected of the client to add an element of unpredictability to the audit process.

Regardless of the level of financial statement being provided to a client and any past relationships with the owners and management, auditors must remain independent, objective, and skeptical, approaching each engagement as if it was their first experience with a brand-new client. Anything less will likely cause the auditors or accountants to miss the fraud.

Beyond Traditional Audits

Financial statements and information are often generated and provided by organizations for reasons beyond annual audits. For example, companies involved in a lawsuit may be required to provide financial information to support or negate a claim. An organization that experiences a loss of any kind may be required to provide a damage calculation along with all supporting financial information.

In most cases, traditional audit procedures are not performed outside an audit, although there often are no limitations preventing the performing of the audit steps. Often, the level of sophistication in a financial fraud scheme is much lower than when committed during a traditional audit. Performing the trend analysis procedures described above on the financial information provided will often identify issues and help determine whether reliance should be placed on the information. Corroborating the financial information between one source and another could also identify reliability issues, such as reconciling results and amounts between the financial reports and the entity's tax returns.

Case Study 3.3 – Asset-Based Lending (ABL) Fraud

A company has limited means to borrow funds. A mortgage exists on the building, and there are outstanding loans on the equipment and vehicles. Yet the company requires more cash flow to fund operations. Many banks have asset-based lending programs available, whereby the company can borrow against their eligible accounts receivables and inventory. The bank defines what constitutes eligibility, and

(Continued)

the company can borrow amounts up to a set borrowing limit, based on accounts receivables and inventory on hand.

To ensure the accounts receivable and inventory amounts are valid, banks often use internal auditors as well as external auditors to visit the customer's location and independently verify the existence of the receivables and inventory. Procedures that are similar, if not identical, to traditional audit procedures are performed in these areas, and the bank receives assurance that the customer's collateral is valid and creditworthy. The process is often termed a collateral review.

I was assigned, along with a colleague, to complete a collateral review of a local manufacturer. Before contacting the customer, we requested and received the monthly financial information provided to the bank by the customer for the past year or more. The monthly borrowing base certificates, the form used by the customer to certify that the amounts reported were complete and accurate, were provided, as were the periodic inventory and accounts receivable reports. We also received a copy of the company's latest corporate tax return.

We determined the customer's borrowing eligibility was limited to outstanding customer balances (receivables) less than 60 days outstanding, along with raw material inventory purchased in the last 12 months. The company did not have any significant work in process or finished goods inventory. The maximum borrowing the company could obtain through ABL was $1.5 million.

The first issue we identified related to the customer's tax return. Although the bank lent the customer funds based on their inventory on hand, the company reported no inventory on their tax returns.

We contacted the customer and scheduled a visit to perform the procedures. We asked them to have their monthly internal financial reports available, including detailed monthly inventory and accounts receivable reports.

When we arrived at the company, we asked for a tour of the facility. As we walked throughout the plant, we noticed raw material inventory throughout the shop. We asked the customer about the materials, their approximate values, and how they were used in their processes.

Next, we began reviewing the monthly accounts receivable aging reports. Using the totals for each month, we entered the amounts into a spreadsheet, tracking the aging buckets (current, 30 days, 60 days …) for each month. After entering the first few months, we noticed that the customer's balances never seemed to get older than 60 days. Using the horizontal trend analysis, we created line graphs of the receivable buckets across the entire period. We wondered how this company could contain every customer receivable to below 60 days.

Without raising suspicions, we completed our two-year analysis. We asked the customer for monthly detailed general ledger reports, which they provided electronically in PDF files. As we scanned through the monthly transactions within the sales and accounts receivable accounts, we noticed a significant level of sales credits posted each month, followed by additional sales transactions. The amounts and details of the sales credits and subsequent invoices were similar.

The customer had developed a routine to ensure the maximum borrowing could be obtained each month by manipulating the accounts receivable to maintain every unpaid account balance under the 60-day limit. As any

(Continued)

unpaid balance approached the 60-day limit, the original sale was credited (reversed) and then re-recorded using a more recent date, allowing the receivable balance to remain "eligible" for another two months, until collected (or reversed and re-recorded again).

Once the scheme was identified, all of the outstanding balances were traced back to the original sales dates and aged appropriately within a spreadsheet. The end result was the bank had overextended credit by nearly half the outstanding balance. We found that most of the account balances exceeded the "eligibility" (60-day) period and should not have been included in the borrowing base calculation.

Regarding inventory, the customer was expensing its inventory for tax purposes while carrying the inventory on the books for borrowing purposes. The customer was committing an obvious tax fraud scheme to minimize income and therefore minimize taxes. We identified this to the bank, and indicated there was a significant potential tax liability in the event the federal or state revenue services identified the customer's tax reporting scheme.

The bank began to work out arrangements, and the customer ultimately refinanced the outstanding loan with another financial institution. The bank received its funds, and now the customer is another bank's problem.

The point of caution here is that financial statement fraud is not limited to audited financial statements. Any financial information, regardless of whether it is audited, reviewed, compiled, or simply produced by a client, is susceptible to fraud and manipulation. Regardless of why financial information is provided, measures need to be implemented and procedures need to be performed to ensure the information is reasonably complete, accurate, and reliable.

Note

1. *Ten Things about Financial Statement Fraud, Second Edition.* A review of SEC enforcement releases (Deloitte Forensic Center: December 2008)

CHAPTER 4

Employee Embezzlements

The Association of Certified Fraud Examiners (ACFE) 2008 *Report to the Nation on Occupational Fraud & Abuse* found that 88.7% of the fraud cases reported were related to asset misappropriation, or employee embezzlement, with an average loss of $200,000.[1] The same study also found that below-manager employees committed the greatest percentage of employee theft at 39.9%, compared to 37.9% by manager-level employees and 22.2% by owners or high-ranking management members.[2]

In a similar study conducted in 2008 for not-for-profit organizations by BDO Seidman, LLP, cash thefts, briberies, and kickbacks were the most common fraud schemes reported.[3] One-third of the reported frauds related to the theft of cash, with an average loss of $45,527. Interestingly, the study showed that males committed the same percentage of cash thefts as female employees, with the highest percentage committed by individuals in the 40-to-49 age group (35%). While only 16% of the responding organizations reported a fraud during the period, a total of 338 fraud cases were attributable to 61 organizations, resulting in more than 5 fraud schemes committed against each organization.[4]

The question posed to me most often is whether there are more people stealing from their employers today, especially in light of the declining economy. To answer this question, we need to look at why employees embezzle. According to the ACFE study, 39% of the cases involved perpetrators living beyond their means, followed by 34% experiencing insurmountable personal financial difficulties.[5] Similar results were reported within BDO Seidman's survey, with 28% of cases relating to financial issues or pressures and 16% to maintain lifestyles. Another 11% reported the motivator was related to a gambling problem. In contrast, PricewaterhouseCoopers' 2007 survey reported that perpetrators chose "financial incentive or greed" to rationalize their fraudulent behavior 57% of the time, followed by "low temptation threshold" (44%), "lack of awareness of wrongdoing" (40%), "expensive lifestyle" (36%), "denials of financial consequences" (26%), and "career disappointment" (12%).[6]

Based on my personal experience as a fraud examiner specializing in preventing and investigating employee embezzlements for the past 20 years, I believe employee fraud and theft is higher today than when I started in this field. I also predict fraud schemes will only continue to increase at least into the near future, due to the declined state of the global economy, the diminished real estate market, the growing unemployment figures, and the overall state of society. Coupled with the perception of no real consequences beyond termination of employment and perhaps probation if criminally prosecuted, employee embezzlement has become a genuine risk to every employer, regardless of the workforce employed. More individuals today have the ability to rationalize their behavior, rather than choosing right versus wrong, and this practice is trickling down to future generations. Lastly, individuals today deny their involvement even when it is obvious and take no responsibility for their actions. Instead, they focus on ways to deflect blame to others. At least, these are my impressions, based on my first-hand experiences.

Case Study 4.1 – Elective Surgery Costs Employee Her Freedom

The physician owner of a plastic surgery center recognized things weren't financially in order and started looking into past bank statements to determine what was happening with the practice's finances. Soon after receiving the bank statements, he realized there were ATM withdrawals, many of them, on the business account. The problem was that he was unaware the practice even had ATM cards for the account. The statements reflected many ATM withdrawals in amounts less than the $400 limit on the same day, often at ATMs located within one of the two casinos in the state. Troubled by his findings, and convinced that the practice's cash (in essence, his cash) had been diverted by one of his employees, he initiated a criminal investigation along with civil proceedings.

Besides the owner, the practice had three regular employees, including a business manager. The two clinical staff members did not have any access to receipts, disbursements, payroll, or bank accounts, so his focus immediately turned toward his business manager. She explained that someone outside of the practice had likely obtained the practice's banking information, created a fictitious ATM card, and withdrew the funds. The owner asked the business manager why the unauthorized ATM withdrawals were never identified to him as part of the monthly bank reconciliations, and the business manager had no response. It wasn't long before the police obtained the video recordings from the casinos and told him that the practice's business manager had made the ATM withdrawals at the casinos. The business manager was immediately terminated.

(Continued)

After months of reconstructing the practice's accounting and banking activity, at a steep cost in professional fees, the owner was faced with embezzlement losses of nearly $500,000. The business manager was arrested and charged with first-degree larceny along with forgery. The business manager was presented with the video footage, along with the financial and banking records of the practice and her own personal accounts. ATM withdrawals from the practice accounts aligned perfectly with deposits made into her personal account in many instances.

In response to the findings, the business manager stated that the transactions and activity were not what they appeared to be. She stated that the transactions and withdrawals were only completed under the direction of the owner in an elaborate scheme to underreport the practice income and minimize federal income taxes. The practice manager stated that the owner had instructed her to withdraw cash from the practice accounts, pay vendor invoices with cash, and deposit any remaining cash into her personal account for future vendor payments. When asked to produce any supporting invoices or other documentation to corroborate the explanations, the business manager could not provide any documents.

The business manager then stated that things far worse than diverting receipts for tax purposes were occurring within the practice. The business manager accused the physician of performing medical procedures under less than sterile conditions and inappropriately discarding used medical supplies. She stated that her concern was for the safety of the patients and the general public due to the issues identified, and that the practice should be shut down for inappropriate health practices pending investigations by the Attorney General's office, the Department of Health, and the

American Medical Association. She was convicted of embezzlement and forgery and went off to jail.

The Fraud Triangle

How do you predict where employee fraud or embezzlement
are likely to occur? The answer lies within individuals who
possess all three corners of the fraud triangle, displayed in
Figure 4.1.

With the exception of career white-collar criminals, who may
go from job to job with the sole intention of stealing from the
next employer, most embezzlers start out performing their job
honestly, accurately, and with integrity. While they may have
had access to steal throughout their employment, they had no
reason to embezzle. Then, something changed in their life; along
came a perceived financial need they were unable to meet.
This "need" could be anything: higher education tuition, out-
of-pocket medical costs, gambling, substance abuse issues, or
simply lifestyle maintenance. What causes one person to cross
the line may not cause someone else to steal. Once opportunity and financial need are present in any one individual, the
last component commonly found is the ability to rationalize the
embezzlement. If you find an employee with all three, it does not
mean they are stealing, but the combination certainly warrants
scrutiny to ensure they are not stealing.

FIGURE 4.1

The only corner over which an employer has any control is opportunity. If someone does not have the opportunity to steal or embezzle, then even if the financial need and rationalization are present, the individual will not be able to steal to satisfy their need and rationalize their behavior.

Someone within the organization needs to assess each position in the company and identify the responsibilities assigned to each position. Once identified, the next step is to determine what opportunities for theft or embezzlement exist, if any, within each position. If no opportunities exist, policies and procedures may not be needed to minimize the risks for the position. However, for any position with identified opportunities, a review is needed to determine what measures can be implemented to minimize the opportunities. Ideally, prevention and detection measures should be implemented, such as:

- Segregating duties among individuals
- Requiring independent reviews over certain transactions
- Monitoring activity and reports for potential fraud or abuse

For example, customer service representatives at a regional manufacturer take sales orders and enter them into the sales system. Orders for existing customers are accepted and added to the schedule when they are posted, as long as the customer has not reached his or her credit limit. The credit manager must approve all new customers prior to accepting any orders, as well as any orders for customers at their credit limit. Customer service reps take and enter the sales orders. They do not handle invoicing, payments, or collection efforts on delinquent accounts. Their only system access is to sales order processing. They do not have access to any other areas of the accounting system. Ideally, controls within the sales order system should be implemented to ensure that customer service reps cannot add a new customer or post an order from a new customer or an existing customer at their credit limit. Without any access to the customer payments, no controls are needed for these positions to ensure the customer service reps don't steal the customer payments.

Conversely, the billing department is responsible for invoicing the customers based on sale terms; collecting the payments; posting and depositing the amounts received; and following up with customers on their outstanding balances. The billing positions typically provide many opportunities for someone to embezzle funds from the organization. The duties within billing need to be segregated so that no one individual performs all the listed tasks, even when other employees are out sick or on vacation. Otherwise, customer payments could be diverted from the company and concealed through postings to the customer's account with little to no risk of being caught. Next, procedures need to be implemented to ensure that all customer payments received are properly posted and deposited to the organization's bank account. Lastly, reports should be generated monthly (if not more frequently) and reviewed to monitor for non-cash adjustments, debit memos, and credit memos posted to customer accounts.

Areas for Concern

While every organization is different, based on factors such as industry, size, and sophistication, they are also very similar in that basic financial cycles exist within every entity. The purpose and nature of each organization will dictate whether certain aspects of each cycle are present. For example, the sales and cash receipts cycle for a chain of retail stores will include significant procedures covering cash register sales and customer returns; the revenue cycle of a manufacturer or a medical practice will likely not address these areas. Similarly, both the manufacturer and the retailer will have inventory issues, but the medical practice likely maintains no formal inventory.

The major cycles found in every organization, in one form or another, include the following:

- Sales (including sales returns)
- Cash receipts
- Purchasing
- Inventory
- Cash disbursements
- Payroll
- Financial reporting

In very basic terms, every organization makes deposits, writes checks, and pays their employees. At the very minimum, it is incumbent for every organization to identify the primary financial areas and assess the level of controls, policies, and procedures in place over cash receipts, cash disbursements, and payroll, as these are the three most common areas for employee theft and embezzlement. A measure as simple as the primary check signer receiving and reviewing the unopened bank statement each month would have identified many of the fraudulent check and forgery schemes I have investigated.

Case Study 4.2 – Cash Receipts

A local manufacturing firm with less than 50 employees was thriving with business. Orders were stockpiled, and the company had a 12-month backlog on non-cancellable work. The firm was a family-run business, and most of the critical responsibilities were assigned to family members. Customer relations, production, and quality assurance were identified as critical areas to keeping customers loyal for future orders. On the accounting and finance side of things, the company depended on their business manager, who managed two clerk-level individuals. The business manager was responsible for maintaining the company's electronic accounting system, receiving and depositing customer payments, and managing the open accounts receivable aging to ensure consistent day-to-day cash flows.

One day, a customer called with a question on his statement. Since the customer's only relationship with the company was with the owner in customer service, he called to inquire why his statement didn't match his records. Attempting to determine why there could be a difference, the owner generated a transaction history of all the customer's orders and payments. The owner recognized that a few of the orders completed and shipped during the period were not on the report. Puzzled as to why there were missing sales transactions, the owner sat with the business manager to find out more about the report. The business manager had no explanation, but stated that she would look into the differences and provide an answer. Days went by, and the owner was not provided with any explanation from his business manager.

The owner started looking into the separate production system and found the records relating to the orders not listed on the report. The owner called the customer to discuss the orders and the customer indicated that the orders were fulfilled and had been paid. The customer provided the dates and check numbers for the payments. Concerned that if the orders were not showing up on the reports, the payments might not show up either, the owner reviewed the deposit posting details on and around the dates of the checks provided by the customer. None of the payments were found in the system.

(Continued)

The owner contacted the customer again and asked whether he could retrieve the images of the checks, stating that he would pay any costs incurred to retrieve the images. The hours seemed like an eternity, but that afternoon the owner received an e-mail with the check images attached. Much to his dismay, the owner quickly confirmed his worst fear—each check had been cashed at a bank other than the one in which the company held its accounts. The payments had been diverted from the company.

The owner showed the checks to his brothers, and instantly, they presumed (accurately) that the business manager had been stealing the customer payments. The owner called the business manager to his office and showed her the check images. He then asked her whether she had any information regarding what happened to the checks. She remained silent and offered no information. He asked her why the corresponding sales orders for the checks were no longer in the company's system, and again she remained silent. With that, the owner fired her and called his attorney.

An investigation was initiated to determine who was involved in the embezzlement, how long it had been occurring, and how much the company had lost. Since the sales orders had been deleted or removed from the system, if they were even in the system in the first place, only orders with corresponding payments and deposits remained in the accounting system. Therefore, the investigation centered on a comparison of the production system to the accounting system to identify all the missing sales orders. Once identified, the missing sales orders were sorted by customer. Each customer was contacted and asked to provide a vendor history report showing his or her order and payment transactions with the company. While it took several weeks to obtain the information, nearly half of the customers provided reports. The same customers were able to provide images of their payments as well.

One of the checks clearly possessed the business manager's endorsement and bank account number; the account number matched her direct deposit account number. A lawsuit was initiated against the business manager, and access to her bank accounts was obtained through a subpoena served on the bank. The deposit details of her accounts revealed she had been stealing company payments and depositing them into her bank account via ATM deposits. While some of the customer checks were clearly cashed at bank branches, many others were deposited directly into her account.

Although many customers never provided their transaction details, the investigation showed the business manager deposited more than $100,000 in customer payments into her account. Customer check images also showed another $83,000 had been cashed and not deposited into a bank account. No cash deposits had been made into the company's bank account. The $183,000 represented roughly 60% of the missing sales orders from the accounting system. If the proven amount of $183,000 was projected to the universe of all missing sales orders, the loss could have easily ranged between $200,000 and $300,000.

The business manager was arrested and charged with first-degree larceny. After pleading down, she received eight months of house arrest, followed by a suspended sentence and probation. As she had no assets or means of repayment, the company avoided costly professional fees and did not pursue their civil case. The company was able to recover $50,000 from its insurance policy.

While employee thefts of cash receipts have been the area I have spent the most time in the past several years, thefts through cash disbursement continue to come across my desk. Many schemes simply involve employees writing checks to themselves, concealed only by posting the fraudulent checks to the accounting system using a common vendor as the payee. An independent review of the returned check images could have detected these frauds, as the individual's name would have appeared as the payee on all the checks.

Case Study 4.3 – Cash Disbursements

The phone rang, and one of the four owners in the office took the bank's call. Nothing was wrong, but the bank had noticed four large, even-dollar amount checks made payable to the company's controller had been processed during the current month. Completely taken by surprise by the news, the owner nearly fell out of his chair. The four checks totaled $80,000, close to the same amount the company paid the controller annually.

The owner summoned the other owners in the building and shared the information. Then they called the controller into the conference room to confront him with the news. The owners first asked him what the checks were about, and when he didn't respond, the owners got angry and started yelling at him. Then they threw him out of the building without giving him time to go to his desk.

The owners called the company's attorney and its accountants. That afternoon, they searched the controller's office for records and any evidence of what he had been doing. They looked for the bank statements and the payroll records, and although they were able to locate many of the records with the aid of the senior accountant, there were gaps in the information located. A quick scan of the controller's payroll for the current year revealed unauthorized bonuses paid at various times throughout the year. These bonuses were made at times when the company was struggling financially and laying off portions of their workforce.

The controller had been with the company for four years, so four years of bank statements and payroll registers were collected. The bank returned the actual cancelled checks each month, but the checks were not together with the statements. The senior accountant stated that the controller received the monthly bank statements directly from the mailman, would open and remove the cancelled checks, and would provide her a copy of the bank statement each month to perform the bank reconciliation.

In matching the actual cancelled checks on hand with the checks listed as returned on the bank statements, the investigation found that three to four checks were missing each month, but each of the missing checks was included on the company's cash disbursement journals. A search of the accounting system for the four-year period revealed no checks payable to the controller. Replacement images were requested from the bank for each of the missing checks, and payroll registers were requested from the payroll service for those missing from the binders.

After days and, in some cases, weeks of waiting for the images, all of the checks were received from the bank. Each check was payable to the controller. Further, the checks were processed in a different font from the normal computer-generated checks. Each check was matched to the corresponding entry in the accounting system, and while each physical check had been made payable to the controller, other vendor names had been used to post the checks into the system. The missing payroll registers revealed

(Continued)

further unauthorized bonuses and extra compensation to the controller.

When the checks, bonuses, and additional compensation paid to the controller was totaled, the loss to the company approximated $1.3 million over the four-year period. The controller was arrested and received a four-year jail sentence, followed by probation. The company did not maintain employee dishonesty coverage, and the only assets found for the controller provided little to no means for recovery.

Desperate people take desperate measures to steal the funds needed to satisfy their financial needs. In the cases I have investigated, I have seen a spike in payroll-related thefts in recent years. The payroll cycle in many organizations does not incorporate a proper segregation of duties. Even if an independent review of payroll is completed, it is often a cursory review at best. Focus needs to be on gross *and* net pay amounts, especially for the individuals with access to process payroll.

Case Study 4.4 – Payroll

A closely held company provided transportation services to private organizations and to municipalities. Individual drivers were paid hourly wages ranging from $7 to $12 per hour, depending on their level of experience and the vehicles they operated. The drivers completed daily timesheets identifying the vehicles, trips, mileage, and time for each day. The timesheets were turned in to the individual responsible for processing, who reviewed each driver's timesheet and used these records as her source for entering each employee's hours into the payroll system.

The payroll person also added new drivers, entered any changes needed for existing drivers, and terminated drivers from the system once their employment ended. Week after week, year after year, the payroll was processed the same way. The payroll person had been with the company for nearly 20 years.

One day, the company's outside auditor was reviewing a payroll journal as part of the audit procedures when he noticed a driver was being paid at the rate of $70 per hour. Instead of being paid $280 for the week, the driver was paid $2,800. When the auditor showed the discrepancy to the payroll person, she acted as if it was the first time she had noticed such a mistake. She reviewed the register and rationalized that she must have made an entry error when transmitting payroll that week, and in place of paying the driver $7 per hour, she accidentally paid him $70 per hour.

Interestingly enough, although the discrepancy had occurred weeks ago, neither the payroll individual nor the driver had ever noticed the overpayment or made any effort to return the excess funds. The auditor collected all the payroll registers for the year, as well as the driver's personnel file. The review revealed the driver had been driving for the company for three years. Sometime during the beginning of the current year, a change had been made to the driver's rate of pay, increasing it from $7 to $70 per hour. The auditor compiled an Excel spreadsheet listing each check the driver was paid since the change, and the gross amount of the checks was totaled. Then the correct rate was applied to the actual hours worked, and the correct gross amounts were calculated for each check.

At the end of the analysis, the company had paid that one driver more than $70,000 in compensation, and had also paid

(Continued)

payroll taxes on the overage. The payroll person stated that she had never noticed the overpayments week after week even though she was the one who reviewed the weekly payroll registers and was responsible for summarizing each payroll for posting into the accounting system. The driver was questioned; he stated that he had never realized he was overpaid. He also stated that he had spent the funds and had no means of repayment.

A background investigation was conducted on both the payroll person and the driver, and it was found that the driver was not related to the payroll person. Nothing unusual was found in either background investigation, yet the auditor felt that there must have been more to the scheme than the clerical error explanation provided. The company agreed and continued its own investigation into the matter and the individuals involved. Although it is highly likely that the two individuals were in collusion to split the overpayment or perpetrate some other scheme to defraud the company, nothing criminal or civil was ever filed for the $70,000 overpayment, and both employees retained their employment with the company.

Unfortunately, in today's business environment, no organization with employees can afford to let its guard down when it comes to preventing and detecting employee thefts and abuses. When it comes to your employees, remember the words of the late Ronald Reagan: "Trust, but verify"[7] and remain vigilant.

Notes

1. Association of Certified Fraud Examiners (ACFE), *2008 Report to the Nation on Occupational Fraud and Abuse.*
2. Ibid.

3. BDO Seidman, *BDO Not-For-Profit Fraud Survey 2008.*

4. Ibid.

5. Association of Certified Fraud Examiners (ACFE), *2008 Report to the Nation on Occupational Fraud and Abuse.*

6. PricewaterhouseCoopers Investigations and Forensic Services, *Economic Crime: People, Culture and Controls: The Fourth Biennial Global Economic Crime Survey.* 2007.

7. "Trust But Verify." *Opinions. The New York Times.* Published Thursday December 10, 1987.

CHAPTER 5

Other Fraud Schemes

One goal of this book is to introduce and explain examples of fraud schemes in ways that can be easily understood by readers with varying levels of accounting knowledge and experience. It would be difficult, if not impossible, to identify and discuss every possible scheme for every type of fraud. Due to the very nature of fraud, and the level of ingenuity and creativity often incorporated by the perpetrators to achieve their schemes, the list of new methods and types of fraud continues to grow. Coupled with constant changes to technology, information systems, banking, and methods for processing transactions, existing schemes continue to evolve into new schemes.

Two of the common areas for fraud schemes—financial statement frauds and employee embezzlements—were discussed in the preceding chapters. Fraud schemes can be perpetrated in virtually any setting or context. The types of fraud schemes that pose a risk to any given organization will depend highly on that organization's nature, size, and structure. Fraud schemes affecting one organization could pose little to no risk to another organization. For example, while bid rigging and vendor kickbacks could pose a significant fraud risk to a government contractor, these schemes pose a much lower risk to a local medical practice. Conversely, upcoding, unbundling, billing for services not performed and other fraudulent medical billing schemes would present as serious risks to a medical practice, but have little if anything to do with a defense contractor.

Every fraud investigator's experience will be similar in some regard, but also different in many ways. Although fraud in general has much common ground, depending on the context in which each fraud professional has worked, the schemes and cases the professional identifies will vary. That is certainly the case with my experience. While my experience is based upon a very diversified background, I also know there are many other contexts of fraud for which I have had little to no experience. I also firmly believe that, regardless of an individual's experience and length of time performing fraud investigations, no one individual could possibly possess experience in every aspect and context of fraud—it's just not possible.

Howard Davia, author of the first edition of this book, relied on his personal experiences as a fraud investigator. Although I never had the opportunity to meet him, it is apparent to me from reading his edition of *Fraud 101* and the case studies he included that much of his experience was obtained through auditing governmental entities, government contractors, and schemes common to those entities—areas in which I have less experience. Mr. Davia detailed fraud schemes he had encountered through his experiences, and often supported his explanations with case studies illustrating how the schemes were perpetrated. The first edition was written in 2000, and the schemes he identified are as much a risk today as they were then, if not more so due to the declining economy, supporting the notion that basic fraud schemes have always existed. Only the nature of each scheme has changed or evolved over time. Modified only to maintain consistency in writing style throughout this edition, below are fraud schemes originally detailed by Howard Davia to show how select fraud schemes are perpetrated.

Duplicate Payment Fraud

Almost every company has had the experience of unintentionally paying the same invoice more than once during the rush of business. It can happen very easily. Sometimes when payment is delayed, the vendor or contractor sends a second invoice or statement, and either both invoices are paid or the invoice and statement are both paid. Companies should ensure that payments are not based on vendor statements; they should only pay on original invoices to minimize this opportunity for mishaps. When duplicate payments do occur, they usually happen very innocently on the part of the individuals involved. Most times, duplicate payments are returned by the recipients or credited to the paying entity's account once identified. It is not uncommon for a vendor to hold the duplicate payment and wait until he or she is contacted before returning the funds.

However, when fraud is involved, an employee of the paying entity normally initiates whatever procedures are required to cause one or more checks to be issued to pay the same invoice. Once signed, the duplicate payment is intercepted or otherwise acquired by the perpetrator. If the paying entity's internal controls are weak, the perpetrator can simply take the check out of the outgoing mail and cash or deposit it. Sometimes the perpetrator will telephone the vendor and explain that a duplicate check was inadvertently sent. The perpetrator would ask that the overpayment be returned to the perpetrator's attention. Under today's banking systems, the fact that the check will be payable to either the vendor or the organization usually creates no problem for the perpetrator who wishes to cash or deposit it.

The perpetrator may initiate the duplicate payment using a second copy of the vendor's invoice, which can be obtained simply either by contacting the vendor and asking for one or by photocopying or scanning the original invoice. Copiers and scanners may be used to reproduce any number of supporting documents with little difficulty, such as purchase orders and receiving documents. All approval signatures and initials can be forged. A key to detecting this type of fraud would be to look for folds in the paperwork. If invoices and other documentation are usually received folded in an envelope, paperwork without any folds would warrant further scrutiny.

Sometimes a dishonest employee will conspire with a vendor, in which case the vendor will provide a second invoice, simplifying the preparation of a second check for payment. If due care is taken in perpetrating duplicate payment fraud, the duplicate payment is rarely noticed, providing that the perpetrating employee is not particularly greedy or careless.

Duplicate payment fraud is relatively easy to discover. Investigators should look for identical payment amounts made to the same payee. A scan of payment amounts can be done manually, such as in small businesses, by visually reviewing the disbursement journals or detailed general ledger. More efficiently, duplicate payments can be easily identified by using software to identify and display payments made to the same vendors for the same amounts. The disbursement journal, imported into Excel and sorted, would be one easy way to accomplish this search.

Multiple Payee Fraud

Multiple payee fraud involves two or more payments made to different vendors for the same purchase or service. One of the payments would be legitimate and the other(s) would be fraudulent.

Perpetration of multiple payee fraud is relatively easy, in that, as in duplicate payment fraud, most of the supporting documentation underlying the legitimate transaction can be switched, reused, or duplicated to support the fraudulent transaction. Supporting documentation for the fraudulent payments usually utilizes the same purchase authorizations, purchase orders, and receiving reports as were used for the legitimate transaction.

The multiple payee fraud perpetrators often work alone. A real or fictitious vendor name may be used, with an address or post office box controlled by the perpetrator to receive all payments. Multiple payee fraud is relatively resistant to detection if the perpetrator works in collusion with an employee of an existing vendor. In such cases, fraudsters can use legitimate invoices and mailing addresses.

Multiple payee fraud is not difficult to discover, but it is more difficult to detect than duplicate payment fraud. The transaction undoubtedly would pass most customary audit tests without any exceptions noted. Either of the duplicate payment files would have a fully documented support file that would satisfy most auditors. Also, audit procedures designed to detect duplicate payment frauds would not detect multiple payee fraud, because no one vendor would have more than one of the payments. As with duplicate payments to the same vendor, a scan or import and sort of the disbursements, looking for duplicate payment amounts on or around the same period, could identify the possibility of a multiple payment scheme. Comparing and scrutinizing the supporting documents for common transactions could also help find this scheme.

Shell Fraud

Shell fraud probably got its name from the old carnival game in which con artists very obviously placed an object under one of three half shells, each of which resembled half of a tennis ball. They would then rapidly move the shells around in such a manner that the victim was always certain that the object was under one of the shells and was always sure where it was. The victim then would bet a sum of money that he or she was right. Of course, the con artists were experts at making the object disappear so that it was not under any of the shells. No matter which shell the victim selected, it would be the wrong one. Shell frauds are so called because, like the object under the shells, the item that was purchased and paid for did not exist and indeed never existed. The basis for shell fraud payments is totally fictitious.

A shell fraud is nothing more than an individual generating a payment to a real or fictitious vendor for a fictitious invoice. In executing shell fraud, the perpetrator initiates a fraudulent purchase and prepares the supporting documents and accounting entries, forging any signatures necessary to approve the invoice for payment. Supporting documents might include requisitions, purchase orders or contracts, receiving reports and invoices—whatever is needed to document the file. The perpetrator then submits the approved invoice for payment. Depending on the size of the entity and the level of internal controls in place, a perpetrator can work alone to accomplish a shell fraud, particularly if he or she is in a key position. It is also common for the perpetrator of a shell fraud to collude with an actual vendor or contractor, splitting the proceeds.

Many instances of shell fraud have been detected over the years. The best way to obtain assurance that shell fraud has not occurred is to independently determine at or about the time claimed that the project, supplies, or service had been delivered or performed as claimed prior to payment. Conversely, one could detect shell fraud by simply selecting a payment transaction and going wherever necessary to verify that the item or service has, in fact, been received, delivered, or performed. When inspection is not possible, one could attempt to verify that the items were delivered or services were performed by independently contacting the supplier or vendor. This approach, of course, would assume that the supplier or vendor was not colluding with the perpetrator. In many cases, there will not be a conspiracy, and the supplier or vendor will quickly confirm whether the product was delivered or the service was performed.

Another measure that can be completed is to independently obtain or verify information about the supplier or vendor, which is often easily obtained via the Internet. Reference to telephone directories, Dun & Bradstreet credit directories, an Internet search for any listings, and similar business reference directories could provide the clue that a payee is fictitious. If the vendor or supplier is fictitious, little to nothing will likely be found online or through the business's home state's Secretary of State Web site. In fact, many companies with proper internal controls have a credit manager to verify a new supplier or vendor before they are accepted and added into the system.

Consider the following examples of shell fraud based on actual cases.

Case Study 5.1 – The Refurbished Water Tank

Government investigators specifically looking for shell fraud selected a $5,000 payment that had been made to a general contractor for refurbishing a 10,000-gallon water tank located atop a 10-story building. The contract called for the contractor to drain the tank, scrape and clean the interior, coat the walls with a sealant, and refill the tank with water.

Because the investigators were searching for evidence of a shell fraud, they proceeded directly to the worksite to determine whether the work had been accomplished. At the investigators' request, the building manager, who had signed the receiving report attesting that the work had been done, showed them the tank high atop the building. He laughed, saying they would have a hard time inspecting the work, for the tank was full of water. But the investigators, who were

(Continued)

experienced in fraud detection, had anticipated the problem and engaged the assistance of a technician who was qualified to inspect the work.

The technician rode the elevator to the building's roof and climbed the steel ladder attached to the side of the tank. At the top, he swung the access hatch aside, rolled up his sleeve, reached into the tank, and felt the interior surface. Next, he dragged his hand up along the side of the tank and withdrew it from the water. He held a handful of rusty scale proving that the tank had never been refurbished.

This may seem like a simple conclusion, but many companies and their auditors have been duped over the years by not employing somewhat elementary technical assistance. Think creatively.

Case Study 5.2 – The Phantom Building Services

In an organization responsible for the management and maintenance of buildings in six states, an accounting clerk with access to the financial plans of all the buildings systematically forged the necessary documents to cause payments for building cleaning services that were never received. He would prepare a purchase order requesting a cleaning service and forge a building manager's name. The document would be duly recorded in the accounting system as a purchase in process. The clerk used a fictitious contractor's name and a post office box address, which he controlled. Two or three weeks later, the clerk would forge a receiving report to advise the system that the service had been performed. Shortly thereafter, he would mail an invoice for payment ranging from $10,000 to $20,000. The system, noting that all prerequisites for payment had been satisfied, would generate and mail a check to his post office box. His scheme was eventually discovered by accident, and he was prosecuted for stealing $300,000. Privately, the entity's auditors estimated his total theft was closer to $900,000.

Defective Delivery Fraud

Defective delivery fraud involves the delivery of products or services that are inferior in some manner or were never ordered in the first place. The supplier or vendor (1) intentionally causes the delivery to be defective; (2) does not disclose the defect to the customer, and (3) does not offer a corresponding decrease in price to compensate the customer for the defective products or services. The products delivered may be short in quantity and/or inferior in quality to what was ordered. Defective delivery fraud is common and should be a regular target area for audit analysis.

Defective delivery fraud involves the substitution of lower quality items, lower quantities of materials, less-skilled labor, and/or fewer labor hours than agreed upon by an organization. The substitutions are made by the supplier or vendor without disclosure or agreement by the purchasing entity, and no price concessions are provided for the substitutions. The perpetrating supplier or vendor profits from this scheme to the extent of the undisclosed reductions or substitutions that were made. Consequences beyond the financial implications may also result from these schemes. As an example, defective delivery fraud might involve a building contractor who cheats on the sand and cement mixture used in constructing bridges and buildings. The resulting concrete eventually crumbles, and the bridge or building collapses.

Many times collusion occurs between the supplier or vendor and a key employee of the victim. If the victim entity's employee is dishonest and in collusion with the delivering vendor, then the delivering vendor has nothing to fear—unless, of course, someone independent is proactively looking for defective delivery fraud. A supplier or vendor may try to sneak one past the receiving employee and, if questioned, will likely claim an "honest mistake." History has shown that most frauds start out small, effectively testing the waters, and that once failures in the internal controls are identified and the small fraud proceeds without detection or consequences, larger ones are likely to follow.

Properly designed internal control systems require that a designated employee complete a receiving report certifying that a product or service was delivered in accordance with applicable purchase order or contract specifications prior to a vendor's invoice being processed for payment. However, if the designated employee is complacent or negligent in performing this responsibility, a vendor or contractor may exploit the situation. Often, suppliers and vendors provide gifts or other benefits to the designated employee or lavishly entertain them. The payback to the supplier or vendor is often a perfunctory examination of incoming goods or services received by the employee. The amount, type, size, and frequency of gifts to a purchasing agent or individual designated to verify orders and services can be very telling about the relationship the employees have with their suppliers and vendors, a potential red flag for the company to take notice.

Defects in Materials or Services

Defective delivery fraud can involve defects in products or services. Materials delivered may be defective in quality and/or quantity. Instead of the high-quality products ordered, cheaper inferior products may be substituted; instead of the amount ordered, there may be fewer items included in the shipment. For example, instead of receiving 10,000 of an item packaged in gross quantity as were ordered and paid for, a physical count of the gross could reveal only 9,967 items were actually received. The supplier or vendor relies on the customer not opening and counting the gross shipment. Services can also be reduced below those ordered. For example, if a contract called for time and materials, instead of providing 1,000 hours of service by the highest qualified individuals as agreed and invoiced, the vendor could have only expended 900 hours, and of those hours, 300 hours were provided by an apprentice whose rate equals one-third the rate of the senior technician.

To illustrate further, the following examples are actual cases of defective delivery fraud.

Defective Delivery of Services

A common example of defective delivery fraud involves interior painting. Many companies defer painting interior office space for an interval of five or more years to avoid the disruption of business that it causes. However, when painting is performed, it is common for building managers to contract for two coats of paint to be applied, in order to satisfactorily cover five or more years of wear and to obtain full brilliance of any new colors applied. Of course, the application of two coats of paint requires the expenditure of more labor and paint than one coat; hence, the cost is greater than that for one coat.

The government, which has millions of square feet of office space periodically in need of redecorating, has long been a victim of this variety of fraud. Every so often, a government building manager has become a willing conspirator of a dishonest contractor. On one occasion at a government building, a painter had allegedly completed a very extensive interior painting job that required two coats for all interior wall surfaces. As was normal practice when the work was completed, he sought out the building manager to verify the satisfactory completion of his work, only to find that the manager he was accustomed to dealing with was no longer employed at that building. Nevertheless, he approached the young man who had just assumed the manager's duties and asked that he sign for satisfactory receipt of the painting. He had applied only one coat of paint, but offered the new manager $5,000 in cash for his certification acknowledging that two coats of paint had been applied, stating that the $5,000 payment was the customary amount expected in these circumstances for the job completion signature. Unsure of what to do, the young man said he wanted to think about it, and needed to meet the next day. He later contacted the agency's criminal investigation office, which arranged to tape record the next day's conversation with the contractor. When the painter again offered the $5,000, he was arrested and charged with bribery.

What is especially noteworthy in this illustration is that the painter solicited the new building manager's signature without any concern for what was a criminal act. It was, in his mind, the customary way of doing business. He did not appear to be reticent or concerned about exposing himself to the potential risk of committing a crime, which indicates that he likely had experience with bribing others in the past.

Ordinarily, performing a defective delivery fraud investigation, such as determining whether two coats of paint were in fact applied, will be a problem. Even if it was obvious that only one coat of paint had been applied, the situation comes down to your opinion against that of a skilled tradesman. The problem is particularly compelling if the examination is made months after the work is completed. A fraud investigator must be concerned with compiling adequate evidence to support possible fraud charges against a painter. The investigator's opinion would have very little worth in a court proceeding. Merely eyeballing a newly painted wall is insufficient for alleging fraud or for claiming a refund. In fact, it would be difficult for even an expert painter to conclude with certainty that only one coat was applied when two coats were required. How, then, can people protect themselves in this situation?

The answer is that there is no way an investigator can verify the application of two coats of paint under normal circumstances. But do not despair; there is a way to detect this specific fraud—with a little advance planning. One method for determining whether one or two coats of paint are applied lies within the contracting entity's internal control system. Consider, for example, the control effect if all painting contracts involving two coats of paint were to specify that the first coat must include a certain tint. It is then easy to determine at any time after the paint had been applied whether the new surface includes two coats. A simple scratch in an obscure place would show two colors. Much of the government's painting now includes the requirement that the first coat be tinted to its specification. Another method would be to physically inspect the painting after each coat, letting the contractor know he must have an inspection and a sign-off after each coat.

In addition, the contractor should also know that these inspections may occur at any time, and someone other than the contractor must verify that the job was done. Performing a surprise inspection (or even proffering the threat of an inspection) can be a powerful internal control.

Defective Delivery of Goods

Suppliers and vendors can also cheat by delivering fewer products than ordered with the hope of not being detected by the purchasing entity. This scheme can be accomplished in a variety of ways. For example, staying with the paint theme, a paint manufacturer might "short-fill" the paint cans he delivers to customers. Instead of putting five gallons of paint into a can, the company may consistently underfill the paint cans, making it look as if full containers were used and requiring more cans than expected to complete the job. A dairy farmer could dilute the milk he ships to dairies by adding water. In one actual case, a supplier added finely crushed black rock, resembling black oil sunflower seeds, to their 50-pound bags of black oil sunflower bird seed. The birds actually discovered the crime, as they ate the seeds and left the black rocks!

Defective delivery frauds are not always perpetrated by the suppliers who manufacture the materials. Frequently, middlemen are responsible for defective delivery of supplies. A distributor could ship a customer's entire order, as specified by the customer, to the middleman. However, the middleman or even employees such as the truck drivers delivering the merchandise could divert some of the items and deliver less than the customer's full shipment.

If the individual responsible for receiving is not conscientious and careful in checking each shipment for completeness, a shortage may go unnoticed. For example, a truck driver required to deliver 100 cases of a certain product could only deliver 98 cases. If the shortage is noticed, the truck driver can readily acknowledge it and offer a plausible explanation. He or she may even find the other two cases intentionally hidden within the other freight still in the truck. Of course, the truck driver could be involved in a scheme with the victim's receiving dock personnel. If that were the case, when the 98 cases are delivered, the receiving dock personnel would sign as if all 100 cases were delivered. If the victim's internal control system is not properly designed and monitored, the missing cases will remain a mystery, and warehouse theft will most likely be suspected.

An actual example of this occurred in a warehouse, but was accidentally discovered during a shopping trip! The theft was discovered when an alert internal auditor on his day off happened to be shopping for bargains at a surplus sale in a commercial warehouse. While examining surplus furniture he noticed several new desks that he liked. Upon examining them further he noticed that the cartons bore standard government federal stock numbers (FSNs). He decided to purchase one. When he returned to work the next day, he researched the FSN numbers and learned that the furniture items had only recently been introduced into the government's supply system and had never been sold as surplus. Further investigation revealed a conspiracy between the freight carrier and the receiving dock personnel. The discovery of the scheme solved a long-standing mystery and explained discrepancies that had been noted for several years between physical inventory counts and the computerized inventory. It had long been suspected that the shortages were attributable to thefts from warehouse stock and defective shipments.

Defective Delivery of Labor

This fraud involves the substitution of less-qualified laborers than specified and invoiced. When an entity contracts for a specific category of skilled labor and is invoiced for that skill level, but actually receives a skill level lower than that purchased, that is defective delivery of labor fraud. For example, if an entity contracts for electrical work to be performed with an electrical contractor and specifies estimated hours of work to be performed by a master electrician at an hourly rate of $75 per hour, any work performed by an electrician or apprentice of a lesser skill level but billed at the master electrician's rate would be fraud. Consider the following case.

Case Study 5.3 – Contract Wage Costs Fraudulently Increased

A large computer software company was contracted to provide system engineers to design a sophisticated new system. It was agreed that the contractor would be reimbursed on a time and materials basis. The contract price was determined based of the estimated number of hours required at agreed-upon hourly rates for the various skill levels of computer engineers who would be assigned to do the work. Senior engineer hours would be reimbursed at $150 an hour, intermediate engineers at a rate of $100 an hour, and junior engineers at a rate of $75 an hour. The contract reserved the right to examine the contractor's records, and the rates included the vendor's overhead and profit.

When internal auditors examined the computer company's records, they discovered that computer engineer skill classifications for certain engineers were all correctly billed. However, they also found two junior engineers billed at $100 an hour who should have been billed at the $75 rate. The actual fraud involved hundreds of thousands of dollars, and the software vendor, a nationally known company, was prosecuted and convicted.

Defective labor frauds are hard to prove unless you have access to the vendor's personnel and payroll records to document the experience level of employees and their actual time incurred on the project. Often the vendor's management is perpetrating the fraud, and the field employees have no knowledge they are being billed out at a higher rate. Proof of professional certifications, licenses held, or educational degrees should be requested for contracts requiring specialized qualifications before the project begins to see whether the rates being charged are appropriate to the qualifications being asserted.

Defective Delivery of Building Construction

Over the years, there have been many examples of building construction contractors who have substituted inferior materials or taken other money-saving but harmful shortcuts in constructing the supporting walls and supports of buildings and bridges. When the buildings and bridges fail, the loss of life can be catastrophic and the architects and contractors involved are disgraced. Of course, these situations normally come to the public's attention only when the structures fail.

Case Study 5.4 – Building Construction Quality Degradation

A high-rise building was found to contain several serious defects, the most onerous of which was that the poured concrete walls of the structure had been cold-poured, whereas the construction contract required that the concrete walls be poured continuously. When concrete is poured continuously, all of the concrete—regardless of how much is poured—fuses together to form one solid, very strong, block of material. This method is most desirable for concrete walls because it maximizes their structural strength. The process is expensive, as much concrete must be poured, causing considerable overtime and night differential wages to be paid over as many days as necessary to finish the wall.

The alternative method is cold-pouring the concrete. Basically, this means the concrete is poured into the forms

(Continued)

---

until a convenient time to stop is reached. This may be at the end of a regular workday or at the point when it is necessary to erect additional forms. The concrete pouring process is resumed the next day or when the additional forms are ready. The problem is that the concrete poured the first day hardens before the next day's concrete can be poured. When pouring is resumed the next day, it is poured on top of the previous day's pour. Where the two pours meet, no fusing occurs, and a fault line is created. In effect, what happens is that two or more huge blocks of concrete are created, one sitting on top of the other. The fault line between the slabs weakens the structural strength of the wall, and under the right conditions, such as a mild earthquake, the wall can unexpectedly collapse. Conversely, if it is continuously poured, the wall should never fail. Fault lines, especially in buildings more than ten stories high, are very serious in regard to the structural soundness of the building. In this particular case, the building contractor further weakened the walls by discarding scrap lumber into the wet concrete mix. Even when the fraud was detected, the building's owner chose never to pursue the defective delivery, because it would require demolishing the structure and starting over.

Along similar lines, there was an interesting complication in another defective building construction case. The government required wet-pouring the concrete walls with no construction debris discarded into the concrete mixture. To ensure that the contractor complied with contract specifications, a full-time engineer was assigned to the site to maintain surveillance over the construction process. This assignment required the engineer to travel to the building site from his home, a considerable distance away, and return home each weekend. In effect, the onsite engineer was the quality control representative on behalf of the government. His purpose was to ensure that the contractor complied with all contract requirements. Foolproof? Obviously not. It seems the engineer had a mistress in a third city with whom he chose to spend his weeks away from home. His absence from the construction site allowed the building contractor to deviate from contract specifications. The wayward engineer's deeds were discovered after the building was erected. He was allowed to resign without prosecution after he agreed to repay the travel and subsistence expenses that he had been paid during the period he spent with his mistress. A large part of protecting the company against building construction fraud is to have a quality construction manager and team onsite to monitor materials, processes, and progress on the project.

A variation on defective delivery fraud requires a little advance planning on the contractor's part to include unnecessary specifications or steps in a contract or purchase order. As the product or service is being delivered, the unnecessary features are eliminated. However, the vendor's invoice still includes the cost of the unnecessary specifications, and the victim pays for them. The result is the delivery of a perfectly satisfactory product or service, not likely to raise objections or suspicions of inadequacy from users, but provided at a cost higher than needed. In other words, although a defective delivery fraud may have occurred, the product or service actually delivered is in no way defective or otherwise unsatisfactory. The victim merely ends up paying for unnecessary contract specifications or measures never received. Because there is no defect, unless a proactive fraud investigator is clever, skilled in the specific contract areas, and actively looking for this type of fraud, it will never be discovered, as there will be no complaints. A sharp construction manager would be expected to notice any changes in the contract or payment application submitted by the contractor and prepare change orders accordingly.

Detection Tips

Defective delivery fraud is not as difficult to detect as some of the other types of fraudulent activities. You need to determine that the product or service contracted for or purchased was actually delivered in all significant respects. Doing so requires a review of the contract or purchase order issued to determine exactly what was required and a comparison of one or more of the line items to the actual products or services delivered. There is rarely a substitute for objective verification of the actual delivery of products or services.

Defective Receipt Fraud

Defective receipt fraud is similar to shell fraud, in that victim organizations pay for something they never received. Often, verification procedures similar to those used to detect shell fraud can be used to detect defective deliveries. However, there is a significant difference between the two fraud types. In shell fraud, a fictitious purchase is involved, and detection is normally relatively easy. Nothing is delivered, and often that fact can be determined readily. In defective receipt fraud, a legitimate purchase is involved, and a product or service is newly delivered, but victims do not get the full measure of the product or services ordered.

For example, if a contract called for carpeting an executive dining room, and shell fraud was involved, the dining room would not be newly carpeted, and a quick inspection would quickly establish that the carpet was never installed. In defective delivery fraud, the contract might require carpeting the dining room with $100-per-yard carpeting. The contractor's invoice would indicate that the dining room was carpeted with $100-per-yard carpeting as specified, and the victim would pay the $100-per-yard carpeting price if the substitution of a lower-cost carpet was not detected. But let us assume that the dining room was, in fact, carpeted with $50-per-yard carpeting. Whereas in shell fraud where you would only need to look to see whether new carpeting had been delivered, if defective delivery fraud had occurred, you would have to go beyond looking for a new carpeting installation to determine whether the contractor actually had delivered the $100-per-yard carpeting. You would have to obtain a sample of the carpeting and show it to a flooring expert for appraisal, or engage an independent carpeting expert to visit the site. It would also be wise to independently recompute the number of square yards of carpeting required to carpet the dining room. Determining that the carpet buyer actually received the full quality and quantity of product required and invoiced often requires the services of experts.

Defective Shipment Fraud

Defective shipment fraud involves the shipment of the victim's products or services that are superior in some manner to the items or services ordered and do not include a corresponding price increase to compensate the victim for the higher quality goods or services he/she provided. The victim organization is not aware of the excess or higher quality products or services being shipped or otherwise provided. Defective shipment fraud may involve everything from relatively petty fraud to large sums. Perhaps the greatest incidence of defective shipment fraud occurs in shipments from victims' warehouses. Whereas a shipping order may call for the shipment of 100 of some product, 110 products are actually shipped, or where Grade-B product should be shipped, Grade-A products are substituted by shipping staff.

Retail merchants are frequent victims of defective shipment fraud, which may involve undercharging customers for products.

Retail sales clerks are known to undercharge friends for items purchased, by simply ringing sales at lower-sale item rates. The widespread use of product UPC codes has somewhat limited the practice of this fraud. However, any enterprising thief need only have the UPC code from a cheaper product at the time an accomplice presents an item for payment. The clerk merely scans the cheaper-priced item while providing the higher-priced item. For example, a friend presenting a $220 item at a cash register may only be charged $20 if the cashier friend scans another product's code with a $20 cost, resulting in a $200 loss in revenue for the store. Some merchants attempting to control this fraud routinely have a guard positioned at exit doors to verify that the products sold were correctly charged. Many high-volume electronics stores and big box warehouses employ individuals to check customer receipts and select items from the shopping cart at the store's exits.

In other instances, trusted employees substitute more costly materials or labor than those that were purchased. This fraud type always involves conspiracy between an employee, for shipping or providing services, and the recipient of the supplies or services being purchased. In some cases, victims are defrauded when dishonest employees fatten legitimate outgoing shipments from warehouses.

Active internal controls are the first line of defense against defective shipment fraud. However, active controls are much like chains: They are only as strong as their weakest links.

Accordingly, although active internal controls are strongly advocated to prevent defective shipment fraud, they must not be relied on in isolation. Random auditing, a passive internal control procedure designed to periodically test the effectiveness of active internal controls, is the most effective way of ensuring the prevention and/or deterrence of defective shipment fraud.

Accountants or auditors must periodically perform, on a surprise basis, observations and testing of the internal control effectiveness. Auditors should determine whether control personnel are rotated periodically and should periodically check the materials or supplies in the process of being delivered to determine that they are in agreement with warehouse shipping orders or sales orders. Where services are involved, auditors should periodically match invoices with personnel time cards to determine that the personnel services as billed were correctly charged.

Defective Pricing Fraud

Defective pricing fraud usually involves charging the victim a price higher than the price that was agreed on or falsely representing prices so as to deceive the victim. The fraud often is easily detected by proactive fraud investigations. An inside conspirator is almost always involved. In most instances, defective pricing fraud works very simply. A supplier or vendor and a contracting entity enter into a contract to provide goods or services over a period of time, in accordance with prices set within the contract. The supplier or vendor periodically invoices the entity at a higher price than that provided by the contract, and a conspirator, an employee of the entity, inappropriately approves the invoices. If the conspirator is strategically placed, excessive billings are rarely questioned. This scheme can also be perpetrated without a conspirator within the entity, based on the lack of attentiveness and alertness of the entity's employees, especially if there is a contract to provide hundreds or thousands of different parts or supplies, each one with its own price.

For example, a utility had a contract with a local auto supply chain to provide auto parts for their fleet of vehicles. Each year, a price was set for each item to be purchased by the utility. However, because each invoice involved so many items for purchase, the purchasing department never bothered to check the prices they were being charged by the auto supply company. Forensic accountants later quantified thousands of dollars in overcharges, based on actual prices charged versus contracted prices. The auto supply company would simply charge the agreed-upon rate for the first few months and subsequently raise their rates in the hopes the unapproved increases would go unnoticed. No one at the utility checked the charged prices in comparison to the contract prices for sample items.

Usually, the scheme is more complicated than simply agreeing to charge a set sum for a specific unit of goods or services. For example, the contract will not be so easily verifiable as to stipulate that the price for items ordered will be $150 each or that the services delivered will be charged at the rate of $100 per hour. More often, these term contracts set the contract unit prices at something that reflects the market price, such as the contractor's most current published or catalog price for the items, or for an hour of service, often reduced by a percentage. Accordingly, contract negotiation usually stipulates the amount of the discount allowed rather than the unit prices to be charged.

In some instances, a vendor or contractor simply charges higher unit prices than those agreed to in the contract. Although most internal control systems require someone to review and approve an invoice before payment, many individuals charged with this responsibility tend to trust the suppliers or vendors submitting the invoices, especially if they have been periodically rewarded with generous gratuities by the suppliers or vendors, so they give the invoices a cursory review, if any. This is one of the hazards faced by employers who allow their employees to accept gratuities from suppliers or vendors. Companies at risk are those who do not state in writing their policy on receiving gratuities from suppliers and vendors. To minimize the risks of undisclosed relationships by employees with suppliers or vendors, companies are well advised to adopt a zero-gratuity policy.

Case Study 5.5 – The Disappearing Discount

This particular case began with a visit by a manufacturer to the government's furniture procurement agency to solicit a large furniture contract. The manufacturer had been a producer of furniture for the government in the past and essentially made the government purchasing office this offer:

In return for a furniture contract for approximately $10 million, which would approximate our cost of production, we will waive our normal 10% profit of $1 million on the order. We make this offer to keep our factory busy, recover our overhead, and retain our employee workforce.

The government, which normally warehouses the furniture items offered for issue to government agencies, thought it was good business to enter the contract at the reduced price and gave the manufacturer the contract requested.

During the production period, there were several changes to the design of the furniture being manufactured, which resulted in the need to hold a price renegotiation conference after the furniture had been completed nearly two years later. Government personnel, as well as those representing the manufacturer, sat around the negotiating table as the manufacturer presented its price recapitulation. In addition to total manufacturing costs of about $10 million, the manufacturer added approximately 10 percent, or $1 million, for its profit. The government's contracting personnel reviewed the contract file and saw no reason to question the manufacturer's price summary. The government adjourned the meeting for several days to prepare the final documents.

As luck would have it, an auditor had the opportunity to witness the renegotiation proceeding. He vaguely

(Continued)

remembered the manufacturer's offer to waive their customary 10%, or $1 million, in profit. The next day, he returned to his office and reviewed the audit file on the contract. The auditor was thorough and had saved a copy of everything that had taken place since the inception of the contract, including a photocopy of the document signed by both parties agreeing to waive the 10% or $1 million profit. The manufacturer had substituted a similar document in its file that did not show that the profit had been waived. Interestingly, the copy of the document waiving their profit was also missing from the government's official file. The auditor's copy of the document prevailed, and the manufacturer's claim for its $1 million profit was denied. At the time this happened, the question that seemed to defy solution was why the government's file did not include the document that the auditor had in his file. An unrelated event that occurred six or seven years later suggested the answer. One of the officers of the manufacturer was involved in the prosecution of another firm. During the questioning, it was revealed that the manufacturer had been paying a government employee $500 per month to perform certain favors. Could the same government employee have removed the critical document from the government's files?

In pursuing defective pricing fraud, you should always become thoroughly familiar with the supplier or vendor purchase order terms and specifications. When examining invoices, you must make certain that all the terms were correctly applied to the invoice and that the contract or purchase order specifications agree with the supplier's or vendor's invoice.

For larger contracts, the internal auditors should occasionally extend audit procedures to determine that contract specifications are correct. Auditors should ensure that contract specifications were not altered after the supplier's or vendor's proposal was accepted. This can be accomplished by examining the detailed price proposal submitted by the supplier or vendor when responding to the invitation for bids (IFB), if it is an advertised contract, or by reviewing the records of negotiation if it is a negotiated contract.

CHAPTER 6

Contract Rigging Schemes

A lthough contracts are rigged or manipulated for fraudulent purposes in multiple ways, they always tend to involve a two-stage process. The first stage involves doing whatever is necessary to obtain the contract award. The second stage involves the actual mechanics of defrauding the victim. Contract rigging almost always involves conspiracy between an employee of the contracting entity and the contractor. Where contracts are rigged, the resultant fraud can be very significant in terms of dollar cost to the victim.

Stage One: Obtaining the Contract

The first objective of a perpetrator engaged in contract rigging fraud is to obtain the award of the contract. This step is absolutely necessary if the perpetrator is to gain the opportunity to defraud the victim.

Advertised Contract Awards

Most entities believe that the best way to protect themselves from fraud and ensure that they have obtained the lowest price for whatever it is they wish to acquire is to advertise their intentions and allow the marketplace to respond to their invitations to bid. They then select the lowest "qualified" bidder from the contractors, suppliers, or vendors who responded. The theory is that this practice allows the marketplace to determine the best contract price and ensures that the contractor will be selected impartially. Most entities, public and private, require the use of this advertising process, in the naïve belief that it protects their interests. They believe that interested contractors will sharpen their pencils and, in competing with each other, offer their lowest prices.

In a perfect world, this process probably would work very well. However, we do not live in a perfect world, and the process is flawed. Undoubtedly, many honest contractors do respond to requests for proposals on major acquisitions. However, dishonest contractors are also likely to respond. Dishonest contractors have several ways to submit low price bids and win contract awards. Some schemes involve plans to engage in defective delivery fraud, lowering their cost expenditures by substituting cheaper materials and labor. Others may engage in contract rotation fraud, wherein a number of contractors will conspire to submit bids in response to an advertisement, allowing a chosen one of their select group to submit the lowest bid yet give the appearance of competition. On larger contracts, contract rigging is a favorite practice of dishonest contractors.

Advertised Acquisition Process

When entities decide on a major acquisition, such as a construction project, and are ready to select a contractor, they commonly publish their intentions in a newspaper, on the Internet, or in other appropriate regional media to invite all prospective contractors who wish to compete to make their interest known to the advertising entity. Contractors who express their interest are given information needed to bid, including a complete set of blueprints, related specifications, and all information that may be necessary to allow each contractor to prepare cost estimates. Usually the contractors are instructed to submit a sealed bid proposal. Normally, the advertising entity makes it known that the sealed bids submitted will be opened at a specified time and place. The lowest qualified bidder will be awarded the contract.

Getting the Contract Award

To gain the opportunity to rig the contract, any contractor intending to engage in contract rigging fraud must underbid all other bidders so as to be awarded the contract.

Submitting the lowest bid is rarely a problem for contractors that plan to defraud the project. There are two ways to ensure that the contractor submits the lowest bid. The simplest way, if possible, is to have an accomplice, usually a key individual or relative of the advertising entity, provide information regarding the lowest bid received from the other bidders. The fraudulent contractor must delay submitting its bid until the very last moment, at which time the contractor needs only to revise and finalize its estimates to ensure its bid is just below the lowest bid to obtain the contract award. Bids that are close in amount to other bids are rarely questioned.

To prevent this from occurring, most advertising entities require that all bids received be sealed and opened only in a public forum attended by all interested bidders at a previously announced time and place. In such instances, there is little to no opportunity for an accomplice to obtain information regarding the lowest bid to help a dishonest contractor undercut it.

When dishonest contractors cannot gain the advantage of knowing the other bids submitted in advance, their submission of the lowest bid is made more difficult. However, they still have an advantage because, unlike the honest contractors, they do not have to submit a price proposal that will make a profit. When a contractor is contemplating contract rigging fraud, the profit will be realized during stage two of the scheme. Accordingly, preparation of a price proposal is dominated not by computations of what production costs are likely to be but rather by estimates of what other interested contractors are likely to bid. Perpetrators also ensure that their bids are not so low that they appear totally unrealistic. Many bids submitted by fraudulent contractors would result in their financial ruin if they were required to meet their contract requirements as written. It is the contract rigging fraud that takes place during stage two that garners their profits.

In situations where inside conspirators are sufficiently influential, conspiring contractors have the opportunity to know the prices that other contractors have provided, which gives them an opportunity to adjust their prices after the sealed bid opening.

Case Study 6.1 – "Fair" Rent Bidding

In one large contracting action, the government sought to lease 400,000 square feet of office space for a large agency. The specifications for their space needs were delivered to approximately six property owners who had expressed an interest in participating in the leasing action. Four property owners responded with sealed bids offering satisfactory office space, together with proposed rental rates.

After the bids were opened and reviewed, someone decided that the original specifications provided to the six interested landlords were unclear. To be "fair," it was decided that the ambiguity should be explained and all bidders should be given the opportunity to adjust their bids. A notice was sent out to all bidders with the clarified specifications, and all bidders were told that they would be permitted to resubmit their bids if desired.

It became apparent that the original specifications were not too ambiguous, because three of the bids returned were identical to the first bids submitted. One bidder, however, who had originally bid a specified rate, changed its bid to a lower rate, just one cent under the previously provided lowest bid. The original bid amounts submitted were supposed to have been held in confidence and not disclosed. However, it seems obvious that the new low bidder had been informed by someone of the amount of the previous lowest bid.

Not all low-price bids that appear to be suspiciously low are made with the intention of committing contract rigging fraud. For example, sometimes due to a contracting entity's history of not being able to resist changing contract specifications, a bidder may feel they can predict the contracting entity's future actions and will gamble that post-contract changes are likely to occur. Accordingly, a bidder will offer a suspiciously low price, designed to win the contract award, a price the bidder could never live with were it required to complete the contract without change orders. However, no inside conspiracy may be involved, and there may be no criminal manipulation. Contractors, based on past observations of the contracting entity's impulsive behavior, simply gamble that the contracting entity will continue to tamper foolishly with contract specifications. Naturally, when that occurs they will use the opportunity to revise their price. This approach does not, in and of itself, constitute criminal behavior. If the entity does not change the contract as the contractors hope, they would have to perform as required at the original price bid, and they would probably lose money. These contractors, however, often have a fallback provision that allows them to declare bankruptcy (or do something less drastic), enabling them to escape from fulfilling the terms of the contract.

Many contracting entities cannot resist making changes to a contract after the initial award, in order to incorporate afterthoughts to the specifications. Auditors are advised to review the contracting records of their employers or clients for evidence of this practice and firmly advise against it. Internal control systems should firmly require a no-contract-change policy or one that requires high-level approval by management of all changes.

The first objective of the perpetrator is to secure the award of the contract. Nothing else is important. At the successful end of stage one of contract rigging fraud, no crime has yet been committed, except perhaps the act of conspiring to commit a crime. However, once stage one is complete, the perpetrator has gotten his or her proverbial foot in the door.

Stage Two: Contract Change Orders

Stage two of contract rigging fraud begins after the contract has been signed. Although fraudulent intent may be involved in stage one, it is within stage two that the victim is actually defrauded. The contracting entity is defrauded in a number of ways, all of which involve contract specification change orders.

A contract is a legally binding agreement between two parties. In its simplest form, the contract agreement provides that contractors will deliver a specified product or perform a specified service, and in return the contracting entity agrees to pay an agreed-upon sum to the contractor.

The contracting entity often reserves the right to change the original contract specifications as necessary. When the contracting entity wishes to make a change to the contract, it prepares a document called a contract change order. Sometimes when a product is undergoing specification changes, the change order is called an engineering change order. In the contract change order, the contracting entity specifies the exact nature of the changes it wishes the contractor to make, and the contractor must proceed to make them. However, it is always stated in writing that there will be a cost adjustment up or down as necessary to effect the changes, together with a renegotiation of prices to reflect any cost increases or decreases resulting from the contract changes. The contractor's cost of making the changes is usually fully reimbursable and left to be determined at some point after the contractor has completed the contract. Both parties to the contract are required under civil law to comply with contract change provisions.

Once a contract change order is issued, the contracting entity becomes vulnerable to whatever significant cost liability the dishonest contractor has planned. The entity initiating a contract innocently extends the opportunity for fraud merely by instituting contract changes. What the contracting entity does not know is that often many of the changes are planned prior to the award of the contract by one or more of the entity's corrupt employees. Consider, for example, the pricing advantages available to a contractor who is aware of, and can depend on, major specification changes that will be made subsequent to the award of a contract. There are many ways contractors can adjust a price proposal to obtain the award of the contract and profit handsomely subsequent to the award.

Some of the schemes contractors can perpetrate include:

- Bid a low price on contract items that, they are assured, will be eliminated during the term of the contract
- Defer work on contract items they know will be changed and falsely claim to have invested substantial sums in time and material, for which they are entitled to be reimbursed
- Substitute cheaper materials than those specified
- Unbalance the bid in such a way as to profit disproportionately as items are changed or eliminated

Some entities strictly follow the practice of no change orders after signing. However, most contracts do not restrict changes as a matter of general practice. Where public entities are involved, such as federal, state, and local agencies, officials may have a fraudulent interest in seeing that the changes are made. Other organizations in which the managing officials are not a part of the vested ownership of the entities involved, such as colleges, universities, and hospitals, also may have similar interests and may, in fact, themselves be the inside conspirators who assure contractors that certain changes will be made from which they all will be able to profit. To avoid this fraud peril, the general rule is to not enter into a contract unless you are absolutely sure that changes will not be necessary.

Entities that do change contract specifications are exposed to a wide variety of fraud practices and should beware of becoming victims. Of course, all contract specification changes do not incur fraudulent intent, but all are risky. Obviously there are many honest contractors who will submit the fair cost of any changes made. However, even honest contractors may find it hard to resist the opportunity to recover costs and profits that may have been lost in competitive bidding and cost-shaving.

When a contracting entity decides to alter the specifications of an existing contract, two events occur. First, the contracting entity must formally change the contract's requirements, and second, it must provide for an appropriate adjustment in the contract price. Generally, the amount of the adjustment cannot be computed until after the required change is completed. This is as it should be. However, at this point the contracting entity is at the mercy of the contractor. The contracting entity has lost any advantage originally gained when the contract was competitively advertised, when bidding contractors were constrained in price proposals by competition. Once a contract has been awarded and changes are made, there are no such natural price restraints. The contract change order is, in effect, a sole-source contract. When contracting entities require changes, they no longer have the option of choosing another contractor, and the contractor can, at the very least, be expected to be generous in his or her own behalf in recovering all costs and profits. For

dishonest contractors, being given a change in contract requirements is like being given the combination to the bank vault.

Change Orders to Correct Omissions

It is not uncommon for a contracting entity to fail to include
all features of a construction project in the specification package mailed out to contractors. When this occurs, and when the
omission is not detected before the specifications package is
mailed out to prospective bidders, contractors are likely to prepare their bids for a complete, all-inclusive structure, often by
relying heavily on statistical costs to prepare their cost estimates
(e.g., $100 per square foot). After all bids are received, the low-
est qualified bidder is awarded the contract and authorized to
proceed with construction.

As actual contract work gets underway and specification
omissions are discovered and brought to the customer's attention, the customer has no choice but to issue a contract change
order to include the missing specifications in the contract. Were
the change order not written, contractors would be perfectly
within their rights to construct the building as originally specified, even though the plans were deficient. Contract change
orders covering the missing specifications require contractors to
comply. However, because the change orders specify work that
was not in the original specification package on which the contractors bid, they are entitled to add extra costs to the contract
price. Sometimes the omissions are unintentional, and in such
instances no fraud may be involved.

However, if contractors were aware of the omission at the
time they prepared the price proposal, this knowledge would
allow them to reduce their estimated price for the construction
and give them a pricing edge in the competitive bid, an edge
that contractors who did not detect the omission would not have.
More to the point, if the omission was not readily apparent, if

perhaps it was intentionally omitted, and one bidding contractor was informed as to the nature of the missing specification, that bidder would have a clear advantage over other bidders. Such information would enable that contractor to underbid the others, knowing that there would be a later opportunity to add back any costs that were eliminated in the competition to be low bidder.

Experienced accountants and auditors should view all contract change orders warily. They should be concerned immediately about whether the omission was accidental or planned. If the omission appears to have been planned, fraud bells and whistles should begin to sound, and the entire contract should be considered suspect and require a critical examination.

Assuming there were no further irregularities in the contract, at the very least, the contracting entity would have lost any advantage received through the competitive bidding process and may end up paying a costly premium for the omission. However, where significant omissions have occurred and the omissions were planned for fraudulent purposes, it would be surprising if the contracting entity did not experience a need for more changes as the contractor's work continued.

Specification Change Orders

Some entities, when constructing a new building, follow a strictly hands-off or turn-key policy. These terms mean that once the contract has been awarded, the architect and/or contractor is responsible for delivering a fully functional building for the agreed-upon price. The entities take the self-protective attitude that the architect and/or contractor should have exercised due care before the contract award. They contend that by submitting the completed blueprints and/or contract bids, the architect and/or contractor became responsible for performance in accordance with them. The entities want nothing to do with construction problems and avoid any involvement with the construction until the architect or contractor gives them the keys to open the completed building. If there is a need to change a specification that was not foreseen by the architect, an entity's attitude could be: "It is the architect's responsibility, he or she should bear the cost." Entities take these attitudes to protect themselves from cost increases, problems of any sort encountered during construction, and the risk of contract rigging fraud. Should any problems result in contract delivery delays or cost claims, they are prepared to enforce the terms of the contract that call for a completed building at an agreed-upon price at a specified time. The downside of this policy is that the architects and/or contractors who accept this degree of risk are apt to charge more for taking it, increasing the cost of the construction.

However, few entities can actually restrict themselves to a hands-off approach. Most tend to be drawn into the construction details, changing building features sometimes capriciously and exposing themselves to a multitude of abuses. Sometimes their changes are the result of innocent second thoughts or omissions, but sometimes the changes are premeditated by inside conspirators to produce the opportunity to defraud the contracting entity.

In the following case, consider what happened during the construction. Were the changes honest and sincere, or were they fraudulently inspired? This is a true story.

Case Study 6.2 – The Construction in Progress Specification Change

A six-story building was in the process of being constructed. The contract had been advertised. After several months had

(Continued)

elapsed, the tenant that was to occupy the building stated that it wanted a minor change in the building's design. After reviewing the directional orientation of the property, it decided it wanted to take advantage of morning sunlight through a laboratory's windows, and insisted the building be rotated clockwise on the site about 90 degrees. Because none of the building's foundation or superstructure had yet been built, the request was granted, and a contract change order was issued.

Much later, when the time came for the contractor to submit the costs incurred as a result of the change in plans, they were found to be substantial. The construction contractor claimed he had already installed all underground utilities (water, sewer, electrical), which had to be redone when the building site plan was rotated away from its original site. In addition to claiming the cost of installing new underground utilities, he claimed all of the costs he incurred in installing the underground utilities as originally specified. His claim was perfectly legitimate and it had to be paid. However, the circumstances certainly presented an opportunity for padding his expenses.

A fraud examination was never performed in response to the information, although one would have been warranted. However, had an examination been done, the fraud examiner would surely have attempted to resolve the following questions:

Could the contractor have actually installed the underground utilities that he claimed became redundant when the new contract change order was issued? If he had reason to suspect that the building site would be changed at the start of the contract, he could have delayed installing the underground utilities to the original site and later could have claimed he had installed them, charging for the utilities to the original site as if they actually were installed. How could he be aware of the coming change?

There are several possibilities, all of which would have required a bit of advance planning. For example, the architect may have known that the new building's tenant was vulnerable to the suggestion that the building's laboratories face toward the southeast to catch the morning sun. To take advantage of this vulnerability, he need only design the building with its laboratories facing northeast. It would be very easy subsequently to plant that idea in the tenant's mind. This scheme, of course, would require collusion between the architect and the contractor.

A dishonest contractor would not have installed any underground utilities to the original location site if he was aware of the impending contract change order, and particularly if he was conspiring with the architect. He would simply delay installing the utilities, or even perhaps install the utilities in the location needed to best serve the expected new building site. His false claim would be totally unfounded, but at the time he would be most likely to file it, it would be very difficult to prove it was false.

Was the prospective tenant a conspirator to the fraud suggested here? If the tenant was influential in choosing the building's original site, as can be expected, his or her subsequent change of heart is at the very least suspicious and certainly would have been enabling.

Is there any evidence that the contractor or architect were aware of the tenant's site wishes before the bid proposals were submitted? If so, this information could have given the contractor an unfair advantage in preparing his price proposal.

Consider the possibility that architects may be co-conspirators in fraud by designing or omitting construction features that will subsequently require contract changes and provide the opportunity for costly, perhaps fraudulent claims.

However, you must also determine the general design specifications that architects were given by their clients.

Post-Award Change Orders

Contract rigging with fraudulent intent occurs in the acquisition of personal property as well as real property. Most of the mechanics in personal property fraud are very similar to those involving real property. The fraud usually occurs in the acquisition of items manufactured to the entity's specifications, as opposed to off-the-shelf items. The entity's interest in purchasing custom-made items is made known to the relevant manufacturing community. Manufacturers interested in competing are provided with manufacturing specifications. Manufacturers submit price proposals. The lowest qualified bidder is awarded the contract to manufacture the items. Any changes made after the contract is awarded are accomplished through change orders.

Product Degradation

Surely everyone has seen old movies where someone is given a gold coin in payment for something. The recipient frequently bites the coin to verify if it was gold. Obviously, the recipient is concerned that someone will substitute a cheaper metal for the more valuable gold. Base metals such as lead have been substituted for precious metals such as gold. Anyone who has any doubt as to the profit to be made in substituting lead for gold need only to look at the commodities market on any given day. For example, gold was worth about 10,000 times the price of lead, yet a government contractor substituted lead for gold in a defense contract, claiming that there was no cost effect in recommending the engineering change to the U.S. Navy. The details are relayed in the following case.

Case Study 6.3 – Poisoned by Lead?

This story begins with a contractor who obtained a government contract to build an antiaircraft missile for the U.S. Navy. The initial contract was sole-sourced (given without any competition) to a very capable aerospace contractor to design and build a long-range missile with certain prescribed defense capabilities that did not then exist in the Navy's arsenal. No specifications existed that could be advertised, and as customary in such instances, the contract was fully cost-reimbursable.

The contractor labored for several years, designing and building prototype missiles. Using design recommendations provided by a major university, the contractor ultimately constructed a missile that ended up being very effective, with a high target acquisition rate. As is usual with cost-reimbursable contracts of this type, no expense was spared to build the very best missile, to heighten its dependability in acquiring and destroying enemy targets many miles away from the fleet. As cost was secondary to quality, the highest-grade components were used, including nickel and gold plating on electrical circuit board pathways.

After several years and many millions of dollars spent on design, engineering, and prototype construction, the missile specifications had evolved sufficiently and were enduring enough to justify a large production contract. The Navy, interested in obtaining the best possible production price, decided to advertise the contract and solicited price proposals from several major manufacturers, one of which was the original contractor.

(Continued)

Prior to this time, the contractor had no real incentive to reduce manufacturing costs. Production had not been cost-effective, and the contractor quickly realized that its prior extravagant production experience would be a liability rather than an advantage. If it were to win the advertised contract award, the contractor would have to offer a price that would underbid a very competitive marketplace, which would be difficult to do. Nevertheless, it did. It bid what it believed to be a low competitive price, one that was considerably below its previous costs per missile produced under the cost-reimbursable contracts. Its proposed price was the lowest bid, and it was awarded a production contract approximating $100 million.

However, it did not take the contractor long to realize that it would lose significant money if it was required to build the missile at the price bid. Therefore, shortly after the contract was awarded, a group of the contractor's engineers found themselves in meetings to discuss ways and means of sufficiently reducing the cost of manufacturing the missile to enable the company to make a profit. The engineers suggested various ideas for changes that would reduce costs. Many of the suggested changes eliminated parts, modified physical design of the parts, substituted cheaper materials, relaxed acceptance tolerances and reduced prescribed testing. Generally, the changes served to make the missiles much less expensive to produce.

The problem with the cost reduction changes that were suggested, aside from the fact that the changes would result in a degraded product, was that the contract bid price for building the missiles was based on the higher missile specifications existing at the time the contract was advertised. Any cost reductions that would result from making them should have been passed on to the U.S. Navy and should not have benefitted the contractor, unless, of course, the owners were deceitful, and that is exactly what it appears to have happened.

Government auditors discovered details that revealed the contractor's intention to cut production costs and hence build its profit from its low bid. The auditors' report revealed that the contractor was trusted to designate which engineering changes were higher level in nature (thus requiring a comprehensive review by Navy engineers) and which were lower level and not subject to extraordinary review. This, of course, was a rather naïve internal control plan, somewhat akin to giving a fox the keys to the henhouse. The contractor simply designated many of the engineering specification changes that resulted in the missile's degradation as lower level changes, thereby avoiding scrutiny of its claims that no cost reductions were involved. The changes were approved by engineers at the contractor's plant, without any questions as to the serious nature of the changes or the cost effect. The office apparently had no problems with the contractor's claim that the substitution of a tin/lead alloy in lieu of a nickel/gold alloy plating would result in no cost savings.

The auditors computed a $50,000 savings in materials to the contractor from this single change. In another of the several hundred other changes made by the contractor, the office apparently had no problem approving the contractor's claim that no cost savings would result from the change from hand-soldering electrical circuit board connections to simply passing the assembled circuit boards over molten lead (flow-soldering). The auditors discovered that the change was expected to result in a 94% reduction in soldering labor.

In an interesting postscript to the missile illustration, the Navy eventually became so alarmed at the precipitous loss of their missile's reliability in test firings that it gave an engineering study contract to the same contractor to determine the reasons for the performance degradation. After an appropriate period of time to study the defective missiles, the contractor essentially recommended reversals of the cost-cutting changes it had self-approved and made during the production of the missile inventory.

That was a classic case of contract rigging. The contractor was in a unique position that few contractors enjoy. Not only did the company manufacture the missiles, it also served as the designer of the missiles. Accordingly, it was understandable that when the contractor recommended what it described as minor engineering changes to the Navy, in its authoritative role as the missile's designer, the recommendations were readily accepted. What cannot be as easily explained is why the office approved the recommended design changes as submitted, even though they were obviously not minor and even though the contractor submitted them with the notation "no cost effect," when certainly most if not all of the changes obviously involved labor and material cost savings. Do you smell a conspiracy here?

Unbalanced Bidding

Unbalanced bidding fraud is a type of contract rigging fraud in which a contractor planning to perpetrate a fraud bids a price estimated to be lower than any of the other bidders and on which the contractor probably would lose money if it were required to complete the contract advertised at the price bid. However, such contractors are counting on the occurrence of certain events that will restore profits and more. Unbalanced bidding fraud is similar to the other contract rigging frauds previously discussed, except for one important aspect—it is considerably more subtle, and is often and easily overlooked.

In the other types of contract rigging frauds, perpetrating contractors depend on contract change orders that add new requirements and open the door for price negotiations in which they expect to exploit the customer by charging outrageous prices to recover costs and profit. In unbalanced bidding fraud, contractors anticipate that the contracting entity will cancel a requirement and, as a result, leave them with a handsome profit.

In unbalanced bidding, fraud contractors customarily overprice one or more line items, while they sufficiently underprice other line items so that their aggregate bid is likely to be the lowest bid. Such bidders are anticipating that the items they lowballed will be cancelled from the contract, leaving only the overpriced items to manufacture, resulting in a handsome profit.

The following case study is a very oversimplified illustration of unbalanced bidding fraud.

Case Study 6.4 – A Simple Case of Unbalanced Bidding

Assume that a company wished to have a freight transfer terminal, a warehouse, and a service workshop constructed. All three buildings had to be completed by December 31 of the current year. A penalty of $5,000 per day would accrue for each day subsequent to December 31 that final delivery was delayed. The three contractors interested in participating were provided with the building specifications and instructed to submit their price proposals by line item. The first building was the first line item, the second building was the second line item, and the third building was the last line item. The company reserved the right to change contract

(Continued)

specifications or delete items at any time and to renegoti-ate prices as necessary as a result of any changes it might make.

The contractor price proposals were received, and each contractor was determined to be equally qualified. If anyone other than the low bidder was chosen, reasoning would have had to be justified.

There was nothing apparently wrong with the three bids received. The first contractor offered the lowest price and should have been accepted. This contractor was qualified, and offered a price $10,000 lower than the next lowest bid-der. However, it was learned that an official at the company was aware that the company was growing very rapidly and seriously lacked adequate storage space. This employee had known the first contractor, the lowest bidder, since they were in high school together, more than 22 years ago. At their last high school reunion, she attracted the contrac-tor's interest when she casually mentioned that her company was going to build several new buildings estimated to cost more than $500,000. The contractor was interested in get-ting the job, and the employee mentioned that it would be advertised.

The next day, the contractor called the employee and they had lunch together. The contractor reminded the employee that she had said the warehouse would probably be too small before it was completed, and asked why a larger building was not being built. The employee replied that she planned to recommend just that before the specifications were mailed out for bids. She said that since the building had been planned last year, the company had experienced a surge in manufacturing that predictably would continue. The contractor replied that building a warehouse twice as large would not cost that much more. The employee agreed and said that she did not think it would be difficult to sell the larger building to her management. She said she would begin immediately, to which the contractor replied, "Wait, I've got an idea. Why not wait a few months until after the contract is awarded, and then do it?" He explained his plan to submit a low bid, pricing the warehouse low to get the contract. Then when she was successful in selling the corporation on a larger warehouse, he predicted he could net well over $50,000 when the smaller warehouse was cancelled from the contract and the larger warehouse was added. He offered to split the $50,000 with the employee. The employee agreed, and everything worked according to plan. The contractor turned out to be the lowest bidder.

After the contract was awarded to the contractor, the company notified him to begin construction of the first building immediately. Several weeks later, the employee reported to management that the construction of the first building was proceeding well. She also voiced her concerns that given their excellent sales forecasts, the new warehouse building would very likely be obsolete before it was finished. One of management suggested, "The new warehouse construction hasn't yet been started yet, so we have an excellent opportunity to build a larger building."

Everyone agreed, and building two on the contractor's contract was cancelled and the contract price reduced by the amount he had bid. The employee bought a new car with the $25,000 the contractor gave her.

The company received its annual audit the following January. By chance, the auditors examined the construction contract for the three buildings, saw it had been advertised; the lowest bidder selected, and took no audit exceptions.

Detection Recommendations

Contract rigging fraud, if crafted carefully, is very difficult to detect or to take action against on a timely basis. The important thing, as with all fraud, is to know that it exists and to be watchful for signs of it. Although it is often possible to discern what appear to be suspicious bidding practices or unbalanced bidding in stage one, little can be done to change anything. If a bidder chooses to offer an unusually low bid, one that will lose money, that is the bidder's prerogative. It is not the advertising entity's responsibility to ensure that the bidder makes a profit. However, when suspicious stage one bidding practices or apparent profitless bids are observed, you should view them as possible precursors to fraud. What to do about them is the question. The answer is to watch what may come next very carefully.

In almost all instances where contract rigging fraud is suspected, contract changes are the keys to the perpetrator's success. Stop the contract changes, and you will likely go a long way toward stopping contract rigging fraud. The contract must be changed in some way for the perpetrator to profit. Of course, it is the anticipation of changes that causes the perpetrator to bid low in the first place, as he or she never expects to have to do the job at the price bid. Always remember that as long as the suspect contract remains unchanged, it is very difficult for perpetrators to profit. Accordingly, financial managers, accountants, auditors, or whoever is looking for contract rigging fraud should be somewhat alert to all contract changes, both those proposed before the fact and those executed after the fact.

If suspicious bidding practices or unbalanced bidding are suspected, extra attention should be given to any contract changes proposed by the contracting entity. Such changes should be carefully scrutinized to determine who proposed the changes, the cost effect of the changes, and any other consequences on the overall contract. Every attempt should be made to determine the cost of the change, including a requirement that the contractor prepare an estimate of the likely costs of making the change. Where the changes will have a harmful effect on overall contract cost, entity management should be made aware of the consequences.

If the changes are required because of a design error, you need to find out who was responsible for the error. Was it the architect? If so, they may be responsible for any extraordinary costs incurred. Also, you should make every attempt to pinpoint the source of any changes originating within the entity. In other words, does the contractor have an inside conspirator who may be instrumental in generating the changes? Is there any reason to believe that a contract change was known or could have been anticipated at the time the contract was advertised, one that could have been communicated to the bidding contractor to allow him or her to lower the bid and win the contract? In other words, is there any evidence to indicate when the idea for the change was first conceived? How does that date compare with the bid solicitation dates?

Skeptics who have a reason to suspect contract occurrences but cannot prove anything might consider reviewing past contracts or purchase orders that involved the contractors and/or insiders suspected of involvement. If they are guilty of wrongdoing, chances are a pattern will be evident in past events. Any patterns developed may make or at least strengthen your convictions.

Rotation Fraud

Rotation fraud is a close cousin to contract rigging fraud. In rotation fraud, two or more contractors who dominate an industry in a region conspire to alternate the business between them, thereby defeating the advantages of advertised contracts. They obviously feel that it is preferable to share the business equally rather than to engage in cutthroat competition in which everyone loses profits.

If there are three contractors involved, for example, they will conspire as to whose turn it is to win an advertised contract. The contractor chosen among the group to win will bid a comfortable price with an ample profit, making its bidding price known to the other conspiring contractors, who will then slightly overbid, thus giving the appearance of competition. The contracting entity is pleased and believes it has received the best price available in the marketplace, which is evident in the closeness of the prices offered. Normally, when rotation fraud occurs, there is no conspirator involved within the contracting entity's ranks.

In a variation of rotation fraud, only one contractor participates in a bidding action, conspiring with the contracting entity's procurement agent to provide false documentation giving the appearance that three or more contractors submitted bids. Anyone reviewing the procurement files after the fact will find that the procurement action was advertised, that three contractors responded with bids, and the lowest bidder was chosen. End of story!

It is very difficult to detect or to stop rotation fraud. Rarely is an insider involved, except possibly in the situation just described. All the documentation is genuine, as are the contractors who have submitted bids. One recommendation that is worth pursuing is to perform background checks on bidders to assess whether any relationships exist that may represent a conflict. Another recommendation is to identify all contractors who should have been interested in bidding on this contract. If, for example, a painting contract is involved, auditors should identify the painters in the general area from whom the entity should have received bids but did not. If the list contains more names than those from whom bids were received, auditors might contact them and ask why they did not bid on the solicitation. The potential bidders may never have known about the solicitation, in which case auditors should find out why. There may be political reasons why the contractors did not bid. Perhaps they were intimidated out of the competition. Auditors should get as many details as possible, and follow any leads provided.

Where Do We Go from Here?

Up to this point in the book, we have discussed how large the fraud problem has become, estimated fraud losses and costs associated with various schemes, and discussed in detail different financial areas commonly exploited by fraud. The question that remains is: What measures can be implemented to address growing fraud issues?

Now that we know fraud is a real problem, threatening virtually every organization and social program that exists, it is time to start looking at what has been done in response to the growing size and frequency of fraud schemes, as well as identifying practical approaches that can be implemented to prevent future fraud occurrences. We will also discuss recommended steps and measures an organization should take to investigate known or suspected instances of fraud.

As we move into the next chapter, which focuses on the response to fraud, it is important to keep in mind that new fraud schemes are identified on a regular basis. Areas that historically were not known to have significant fraud associated with them can quickly become the new hotbed of fraud.

Using a current example, the real estate and mortgage sectors have always included some level of risk for fraud. Appraisals could be overstated, applicant's assets and earnings could be overstated, and properties could be flipped over and over, artificially inflating the property's "value" with each transaction. Measures were in place, arguably to varying degrees, to watch for these types of red flags. However, it wasn't until the real estate and mortgage industries virtually collapsed in 2008 and 2009 that the true level of fraud within these transactions became apparent. In response, the Federal Bureau of Investigations (FBI) made mortgage fraud a top priority, creating a task force to focus strictly on investigating these schemes. Lending, too, has changed dramatically, almost to the point where an individual with a perfect credit history and high credit score can find it impossible to obtain financing, due to all the new processes and procedures implemented.

The investment community is the second industry likely to receive numerous additional regulations and oversight in response to monumental fraud schemes detected in late 2008 and early 2009. With losses in the multimillions and -billions, these latest "mega-frauds" have had an impact on thousands globally, and have led to new investigative task forces focusing on investment-related schemes.

Much like the world of medicine, the measures to prevent and detect fraud schemes today are limited to our current knowledge of fraud and only address schemes that are known at this time. However, as quickly as measures are identified to address new schemes, changes in technology and in the way business is conducted create the opportunity for new schemes, requiring even more measures. It is the very nature of fraud that this relationship will continue well into the future.

CHAPTER 7

Responses to Fraud

R esponses to fraud have changed in many respects in reaction to Enron in 2001, and yet much remains the same. In general, fraud awareness is the highest today that it has ever been, but much work is still needed both to prevent and detect fraud from occurring. While great strides have been made in regard to encouraging criminal prosecutions that demonstrate real consequences to would-be fraud perpetrators, far too many fraud cases continue to go unprosecuted or, worse, get little to no attention from law enforcement, prosecutors, and the courts if pursued criminally. According to the Association of Certified Fraud Examiners (ACFE) 2008 *Report to the Nation on Occupational Fraud & Abuse*, 87.4% of the identified fraud perpetrators were never charged or convicted, 5.7% were charged but never convicted, and only 6.8% had convictions.[1]

PricewaterhouseCoopers' Investigations and Forensic Services Division issued their fraud-related survey results, entitled *Economic Crime: People, Culture and Controls—The 4th Biennial Global Economic Crime Survey*, in 2007. They broke down the reported fraud acts by level or position of each perpetrator, with three categories: senior management; middle management; and below middle management. The survey listed the actions brought against the perpetrators, and the highest scoring action was dismissal of the perpetrator from employment, which was the result in 73–87% of all reported cases based on the level of perpetrator involved. Criminal action was only sought for 32% of the cases involving senior management, while it was sought for 54% of the cases involving the low-level employees. Civil actions came in at 33% for senior management and 29% for low-level employees.[2]

A copy of the report, along with much more information, can be found on the ACFE's Web site, located at www.acfe.com.

Unfortunately, unless the fraud case is egregious in nature or the amount involved, or there is some other compelling issue present for pursing the fraud case criminally, the typical remedy chosen by the victim is to terminate the perpetrator, recover the funds to the extent possible through any insurance coverage in place, and attempt to recover stolen funds and investigative costs from the perpetrator through civil actions. In some cases, there is no choice but to involve law enforcement, such as when governmental funds are involved. In other instances, the insurance policy states that the victim must notify law enforcement in order to collect on a claim. However, most policies stop short of requiring an arrest or prosecution. In the end, unless more fraudsters are brought into the criminal justice system and sentenced appropriately for their crime, the strength of the consequence of being arrested and put into prison will only erode, leading to even more instances of fraud.

Government's Response to Fraud

Until 2001, the accounting profession was primarily responsible for issuing the standards, requirements, and pronouncements for audited and nonaudited financial statements. Coupled with the reporting and disclosure requirements of publicly traded entities issued by the Securities and Exchange Commission (SEC), the existing standards should have prevented more of the financial statement frauds and restatements that occurred.

The language in those standards until that time referred to "management's responsibility" to ensure the completeness and accuracy of the financial statements, as well as the sufficiency of the disclosures. Yet despite all the guidance and requirements in place, a significant amount of financial statement fraud was identified that year. Although financial statement fraud was nothing new, the spike in occurrences, combined with the magnitude of the Enron and WorldCom cases, brought increased scrutiny to the audit process, the accounting profession, and the role of independent accountants and auditors as perceived watchdogs for corporate fraud.

Considerable blame was placed on audited entities for maintaining ineffective systems of internal controls and procedures to prevent and/or detect potential fraudulent activity. Although standards required auditors to gain an understanding of an entity's internal control system and determine the level of reliance they would place on it, emphasis was all too often placed on procedures regarding the balances, results, and disclosures rather than on the entity's policies and procedures that were followed to arrive at the final amounts. Once audit failures were identified, whether the result of fraud or error, the entity's internal controls were called into question.

Once a fraud was identified and investigated, prosecuting the entity criminally and holding individuals personally responsible was often difficult. Civil and SEC prosecution was possible, but actually arresting and incarcerating individuals at the entity who were primarily responsible for "cooking the books" and benefiting from the fraud was challenging. Although it was not impossible, proving the chief executive officer (CEO) and/or chief financial officer (CFO) possessed personal knowledge and intent was an issue, even if it appeared that they had personally benefited from the fraudulent activities.

These and other factors led to new legislation that expanded accounting standard settings and oversight beyond the accounting profession, added new requirements regarding assessments of internal controls, and made provisions to hold individuals criminally and civilly responsible by requiring them to personally certify each financial statement before issuance.

Sarbanes-Oxley Legislation

Due to the significance and impact of the well-known financial statement frauds identified in 2001, starting with Enron and WorldCom, and the unacceptable level of restatements by publicly traded entities, the first immediate change to occur was the enactment of the Sarbanes-Oxley Act. This new legislation, often referred to as "Sarbox" or "SOX," required independent review and reporting of a publicly traded entity's control environment and internal control policies and procedures by the external auditors as well as personal certifications of every financial report by both the CEO and CFO.

Although SOX has been around for several years, and many existing books and articles already cover SOX and its requirements in significant details, this book would be deficient if it did not include a brief discussion of SOX requirements.

SOX legislation sought to reduce the likelihood of fraud by making public company CEOs and CFOs directly accountable for their organization's internal controls and financial disclosures. Senior managers would also be subject to greater oversight from more independent boards, internal audit committees, and external audits. Rather than looking on the new law as imposing onerous requirements, management should have viewed it as an opportunity to take a fresh look at the company's internal controls, to assess its risk of fraud, and to make changes where needed to reduce the organization's overall exposure to loss.

The goal of the new law was for internal controls to be so effective that degradation of the system through fraud was virtually impossible. While it could be argued that fraud can never be eliminated, the onus was on management to create the most effective system possible to prevent it and detect it. Audit firms have been asking hard questions before certifying any management report, as their own review must withstand subsequent scrutiny by the SEC. What does a SOX-compliant control environment and system of internal controls entail?

AUDIT COMMITTEES The first step towards compliance was the establishment of an audit committee. Every public company must have one, and all members of the audit committee have to be members of the board of directors but independent in the sense that they perform no other corporate duties and receive no compensation other than their directors' fees. At least one member of the audit committee must be a financial expert. The audit committee is responsible for hiring and compensating both the auditors and any other consultants.

Directors should be experienced businesspersons, and as many as possible should be directors on other boards. SOX states that audit committee members cannot be "gray directors," insiders or those with a high level of equity interest or other personal or business connection with the company. The external auditors must scrutinize close family relationships among directors or the concentration of power is in too few hands. The chair of the audit committee should, as a matter of policy, keep an open door for the chief internal auditor, the security director, and the CFO, and have good communications with the engagement partner of the external auditor. Since the passing of SOX legislation, many companies have set up hotlines that enable their employees to use various communication methods to report suspected incidents and to hold confidential discussions with members of the audit committee.

CODE OF ETHICS   The next step was the establishment of a code of ethics, which applied equally to frontline employees and senior executives. The corporate culture plays a large role in preventing and detecting potential fraud. Employee attitudes are shaped to some extent by the attitudes of senior management. Where management is seen to be adhering to the highest standards of business practice, employees are more likely to do the same.

SOX required any code to focus on conflicts of professional and personal interest, full disclosure of relevant matters in the company's regular filings, and compliance with government rules and regulations. The code of ethics should be written, distributed, and explained to employees at all levels within the company.

INTERNAL CONTROLS   The third step towards compliance, another requirement under the new law, was that management must have identified and assessed the risk of fraudulent financial reporting within its own operations and the adequacy of its internal controls. This review, which many termed a "forensic audit," looked for weaknesses and opportunities for fraud within the organization's internal controls. Policies and procedures should ensure that all transactions are authorized by management and recorded in such a way as to permit preparation of financial statements and an accounting of assets.

INTERNAL AUDIT   The last step towards compliance involved an effective internal audit function. Considered an essential part of any internal control system, the internal audit team should have the full support of senior management, the board of directors, and the audit committee. The integrity and impartiality of the chief internal auditor and the members of the team should be beyond question. The chief internal auditor should report to a senior officer who is not involved in the production of financial statements and should have direct access to the CEO and the chair of the audit committee at all times.

The internal auditor's detailed operational knowledge was to be coordinated with the work of the external auditor to develop anti-fraud controls. Honest employees inspired by ethical business practices and protected by new whistleblower legislation under Sarbanes-Oxley were encouraged to play their role as part of the internal control system.

Public Company Accounting Oversight Board

At or about the same time, the government created a new accounting standard-setting and oversight body for publicly traded entities called the Public Company Accounting Oversight Board, better known as the PCAOB.

The PCAOB issued a series of Auditing Standards (AS), along with interim standards and rules, to govern the financial audits and activity of publicly traded companies. One standard in particular, Auditing Standard No. 5 (AS5), *An Audit of Internal Control Over Financial Reporting That Is Integrated with An Audit Of Financial Statements*, spells out the auditor's responsibilities for assessing, documenting, evaluating and testing an audited entity's system of internal controls. AS5, comprising 55 pages and having an effective date of June 2007, identifies the auditor's role and responsibility towards financial statement fraud. The language found in sections 14 and 15 of AS5 mirror the requirements of Statement of Auditing Standard 99, discussed below.

Accounting Profession's Response to Fraud

While SOX and the PCAOB addressed the issues regarding the financial statements of publicly traded entities, the Act had little to no direct impact on all the entities and organizations that were not listed on Wall Street. Rumors of having these requirements imposed on all audited financial statements never materialized.

Case Study 7.1 – Nonprofit Pandemonium

Soon after the passage of SOX, discussions continued exploring whether adherence to SOX should be expanded beyond publicly traded entities to protect public interests and safeguard the use of public funds. One suggestion explored whether nonprofit organizations that received any form of federal funds, either directly or through pass-through entities, should be required to comply with SOX. Another discussion was occurring at the state level regarding nonprofits.

Needless to say, nonprofit organizations across the country began to panic in response to these discussions. Nonprofit organizations comprised 20% of our client base; most of these nonprofits received federal funds of one sort or another, and nearly all received state funds. Most, if not all, of the entities maintained minimal accounting staff and less-than-sophisticated internal controls—functional and auditable, and typical of nonprofits, but nowhere near the level required by SOX. None of our nonprofit clients had the resources available to become compliant with SOX, should it be required.

While each of our clients maintained a board of directors, some more formal than others, only the more sophisticated clients had a separate finance committee who also typically functioned as their audit committee. Few, if any, of our client nonprofit organizations were at the level to maintain both committees, and the level of financial expertise on the boards and committees varied greatly. In complying with the requirements of SOX, the form and composition of many of the boards would have had to change, raising the level of financial expertise to a much higher level.

We spoke with our clients and had them begin a self-assessment of their state of controls and procedures while we monitored the discussions at both the federal and state levels. We added more emphasis on evaluating their systems of internal controls, financial policies, and accounting procedures during the audits, and obtained copies of their documented policies and procedures to assess the level of adequacy. The backgrounds of board members were obtained and documented for the files, a task we had not historically performed, and the management letters grew in content through new recommendations in these areas.

Thankfully for our nonprofit clients, the discussions never proceeded any further, and compliance with SOX was never expanded to include them. However, that did not change what the nonprofits should be doing with their internal controls and their boards. The tide had changed, and although the initiative was quiet for now, the risk always existed that SOX compliance could be expanded, especially if a significant fraud was discovered in a nonprofit organization.

For many of our clients, a board member for the organization was also involved in another entity subject to compliance with SOX. Based on their experiences with the procedures being performed to become compliant in their other entities, along with their enlightened view of their responsibility to the organization and the financial statements as a board member, many of these board members required the management of their nonprofit organizations to implement similar controls and procedures, regardless of whether it was required by SOX.

Public accounting organizations, mainly the American Institute of Certified Public Accountants (AICPA) and their accounting standard setters, the Accounting Standards Board (ASB), recognized the need to improve existing audit standards for all financial statement audits in response to the growing issue of fraud. The first major new audit standard issued addressing fraud was Statement of Auditing Standards Number 99 (SAS 99), *The Auditor's Responsibility to Detect Fraud in a Financial Statement Audit*, with an effective date of December 2002. Among other new requirements, the new audit standard mandated that every audit team would meet, prior to commencing any audit procedures, to hold a "brainstorming" session with the goal of identifying all the risks of fraud for the audit engagement, as well as to identify how the audit procedures would address each fraud risk identified.

During early 2006, eight more new auditing standards were issued with an effective date of December 2006 to address internal controls, fraud issues, and the ever-changing business environment. Those new auditing standards were as follows:

- SAS No. 104, *Amendment to Statement on Auditing Standards No. 1, Codification of Auditing Standards and Procedures ("Due Professional Care in the Performance of Work")*
- SAS No. 105, *Amendment to Statement on Auditing Standard No. 95, Generally Accepted Auditing Standards*
- SAS No. 106, *Audit Evidence*
- SAS No. 107, *Audit Risk and Materiality in Conducting an Audit*
- SAS No. 108, *Planning and Supervision*
- SAS No. 109, *Understanding the Entity and Its Environment and Assessing the Risks of Material Misstatement*
- SAS No. 110, *Performing Audit Procedures in Response to Assessed Risks and Evaluating the Audit Evidence Obtained*

- SAS No. 111, *Amendment to Statement on Auditing Standards No. 39, Audit Sampling*

The ASB states that:

The primary objective of these Statements is to enhance auditor's application of the audit risk model in practice by specifying, among other things:

- *More in-depth understanding of the entity and its environment, including its internal control, to identify the risks of material misstatement in the financial statements and what the entity is doing to mitigate them,*
- *More rigorous assessment of the risks of material misstatement of the financial statements based on that understanding, and*
- *Improved linkage between the assessed risks and the nature, timing and extent of audit procedures performed in response to those risks.*[3]

Under these new standards, every financial statement auditor is now required to spend more time with his or her audit clients, documenting, evaluating, and reporting on the client's system of internal controls, financial policies, and accounting procedures. Once the evaluation is complete, the auditors must place more reliance on the client's internal controls, versus the prior common practice of virtually ignoring the client's controls as if they were nonexistent and relying solely on substantive procedures.

Much more information can be found on the new standards and fraud-related matters through the AICPA's Web site, www.aicpa.org.

Internal Audit Profession's Response to Fraud

The Institute of Internal Auditors, or IIA, is the most prominent membership organization for internal auditors. Much like the AICPA for certified public accountants, the IIA has been instrumental in changing internal auditing requirements and the training offered members relating to fraud.

While the IIA has yet to develop a credential or specialty for fraud or forensic accounting, they have developed a Fraud Repository through their Web site. The Repository contains resources to assist members with fraud-related matters. In addition, numerous articles on fraud-related issues are available through their Web site (www.theiia.com).

In 2008, the IIA, in collaboration with the AICPA and the ACFE, issued a new tool entitled *Managing the Business Risk of Fraud: A Practical Guide.* The publication, available free of charge through each organization's Web site, represents an unprecedented collaboration among the three different professional organizations in the fight on fraud.

New Credentials, More Training, Better Awareness

ACFE has played a major role in providing fraud training and education since its inception in 1988. The creation of the Certified Fraud Examiner, or CFE, designation, was initially designed as the overlapping area of a Venn diagram between an accountant and an investigator. That diagram has expanded beyond the initial two overlapping circles to include other specialized skills, such as interviewing, computer technology, and psychology, to name a few. The ACFE has become the number-one international organization for fraud training, with more than 45,000 members in many countries around the world. The CFE credential is widely recognized in courts throughout the world, signifying an individual is an expert in the field of fraud. The ACFE continues to work side by side with the AICPA in developing new programs and tools for CPAs and fraud specialists to support the war on fraud. More information regarding the ACFE can be found on the association's Web site (www.acfe.com).

In May 2008, the AICPA authorized a new credential for CPAs who specialize in the areas of fraud and forensic accounting:

> *The credential, Certified in Financial Forensics (CFF), combines specialized forensic accounting expertise with the core knowledge and skills that make CPAs among the most trusted business advisers. The CFF encompasses fundamental and specialized forensic accounting skills that CPA practitioners apply in a variety of service areas, including: bankruptcy and insolvency; computer forensics; economic damages; family law; fraud investigations; litigation support; stakeholder disputes and valuations.*[4]

Other organizations have expanded their missions and offerings by adding fraud or fraud-related training and specialization to members. One organization in particular, the National Association of Certified Valuation Analysts (NACVA), is a professional membership organization focusing on business valuation and appraisal areas of specialization. In the shadow of Enron, NACVA expanded their training and added a new credential in the areas of fraud prevention and forensic accounting. Today, NACVA provides fraud-related training within its Financial Forensics Institute and offers the Certified Forensic Financial Analyst (CFFA) designation with five areas of specialization, as follows:

- Financial Litigation
- Forensic Accounting
- Business and Intellectual Property Damages
- Business Fraud—Deterrence, Detection and Investigation
- Matrimonial Litigation

More detailed information regarding NACVA's response to fraud training and resources can be found on the association's Web site (www.nacva.com).

Within academia, accounting curriculums are a key target for enhancement with fraud-related subjects in an attempt to influence audit training while students are still in school. Great strides have been made in this area. Course offerings in fraud investigation and forensic accounting, which were unheard of just a year or two ago, are now being offered to students at colleges and universities. Although I am not aware of any under-graduate degree programs focused solely on fraud and forensic accounting, a limited number of forensic accounting programs is currently being offered at the Masters level. One school currently offers two different fraud-related degree paths, emphasizing pre-vention and deterrence or detection and investigation. Students today who wish to specialize in this field have much more information at their disposal, in the way of readings, courses, programs and other tools, than ever before.

Articles, Books, and More Resources

There are more books and articles available today on virtually every aspect of fraud than ever before, and new ones are added every month. The range of information includes designing and implementing internal controls and other prevention measure, identifying and investigating all the various fraud schemes, and studies on why individuals and organizations commit fraud in the first place. The materials address many different perspec-tives, from minimizing your risks for fraud as an individual, a lender, an investor, or a business owner to name only a few, through what to do if you become a victim of fraud. As new schemes are identified, or as fraud "hot topics" such as identify theft and mortgage fraud are spotlighted, individuals with spe-cialized training and experience in the areas are writing articles, books, and courses to address the issues.

The availability of information and resources really changes today's playing field. Individuals and organizations are better prepared today to prevent or detect fraud at its earliest stage and have the requisite knowledge on how to quickly and appropriately respond if fraud is detected.

Additionally, attorneys, law enforcement, prosecutors, judges, and juries are more knowledgeable about financial crimes and fraud schemes today than ever before, which helps to ease the process of having a case investigated once one is identified. However, more education and experience are still needed to bring the level of knowledge to a consistent level. While many individuals in these groups have become extremely well-versed in fraud schemes, too many others have done little to expand their knowledge. In certain instances, their understanding may even be inaccurate. Worse still are the individuals who want nothing to do with fraud-related cases. It is a problem that no certain measure is available to ensure that the individual assigned to your fraud case is the person most knowledgeable and interested in financial fraud cases. In some cases, you can make a request (which may or may not be accommodated), but in many cases, it is the luck of the draw.

Case Study 7.2 – No Two Are the Same

I had two commercial litigation cases pending in civil courts. In the first matter, the majority shareholder of a business, acting as president of the company, was using the company's funds as his personal checkbook, along with making poor business decisions to the detriment of the business and his partners. The minority shareholder hired counsel, and after discussions broke down between the parties, litigation was

(Continued)

initiated. I was engaged by the attorney representing the minority shareholder, and my main charge was to gain access to the books and records to determine independently for the court what had transpired with the majority shareholder. To the extent measurable, I was also charged to quantify damages, if any, caused to the company's performance and/or value due to the actions and decisions of the president.

As is typical of these cases, I tried endlessly to gain access to the books and records controlled by the president. Meeting after meeting, hearing after hearing, next to nothing was produced.

Finally, I obtained minimal documentation regarding the operations, and from the information I was able to identify that much of the other financial information, which I knew existed, had yet to be produced. After I shared these findings with the attorney, a hearing was scheduled to enlighten the judge and seek sanctions for the president's failure to comply with production orders issued by the judge.

In describing the information never provided but known to exist, the judge often addressed me directly while on the stand and added to my discussions information based on his knowledge of business records and tax returns. The judge had a great business background and understood the tax and business implications of the issues I raised without my having to explain them in great detail.

The judge issued his ruling in our favor and compelled the president to produce the information or risk sanctions. Not only did his knowledge of the president's actions help move our access to the underlying records forward, he was already favoring in our direction long before the case was ready to be tried in his court.

My second case was very similar, involving an equal partner in a small business who violated a covenant not to

compete by secretly stealing customers and customer information for her separate company and looting company funds
for personal purposes. In this case, however, I was working
for the attorney representing the partner who was victimized,
and she was in control of all the records.

The client was able to identify all the instances of personal expenses being paid through the business, concealed
through fictitious descriptions that appeared to legitimize
each transaction. The client was also able to identify the customers who had been diverted away from the business and
quantify the amount of business that each diverted customer
represented.

I was charged with identifying other accounts and activity beyond those known, to determine what other activity
had occurred at the hands of the partner, along with quantify-
ing the business that had been lost due to customers leaving
the company.

I identified transfers and transactions within the business checking account with other accounts not known by
the client. One of the accounts I identified with significant
activity was a PayPal savings account. Not only did the client
have no knowledge of the account or the business purpose for any transactions with the account, the client had
no records for this account.

I also identified credit card payments to cards beyond
those known to the client. Once again, there were no
monthly credit card statements available for the credit card
accounts although payments were made by the business to
the cards.

The attorney scheduled a hearing to procure the bank
account information and statements along with the credit
card statements. In this case, the judge was an older,

(Continued)

semiretired judge. After listening to counsel arguments back and forth on the matters, the judge finally asked that I take the stand and explain my findings.

I described the limited procedures I had performed to date and the bank accounts I had identified. I also explained that I could not proceed as I did not have the bank information or monthly statements for the identified accounts that would shed light on the activity. I identified one of the accounts as a PayPal savings account.

I could tell the judge had no idea what I was describing. I, then, explained to the judge that PayPay was linked with eBay, the online auction site, and that most often eBay users establish PayPal accounts to facilitate payments for items they purchase through eBay. However, in this case, the account was an actual PayPal bank account used to transfer funds between the business account, and the nature of the business had no use or activity with eBay.

I lost the judge somewhere shortly after indicating I had identified other accounts. The judge stated he did not have a computer at home and was unfamiliar with the whole Internet thing, let alone the eBay thing that I had described.

Desperate to ensure that the judge ruled in our favor and provided us access to the undisclosed accounts and credit card information, I told the judge the accounts were merely additional bank and credit card accounts that had undisclosed activity with the company's known bank account, and that without gaining access to those accounts' information, I would be unable to complete the analysis for the court. I knew it had worked when the judge simply asked me what I needed.

The judge ruled in our favor and ordered that the partner, in whose name all the accounts had been established, find a way to obtain and provide the account statements and

> activity to me to complete my analysis. I am convinced that had I not changed my strategy and brought the discussion back to a very basic understanding for his benefit, the judge would not have acted that day, further delaying resolution to the matter and wasting a day in court.

Now that we've discussed different measures that have been implemented to help prevent future financial crimes and frauds from occurring, we will continue by discussing in Chapter 8 the measures an entity can implement to prevent and detect instances of fraud. An organization's system of internal controls is its first and best line of defense in the battle on fraud.

Notes

1. Association of Certified Fraud Examiners (ACFE), *2008 Report to the Nation on Occupational Fraud and Abuse.*
2. PricewaterhouseCoopers Investigations and Forensic Service, *Economic Crime: People, Culture and Controls: The 4th Biennial Global Economic Crime Survey.* 2007.
3. Statement on Auditing Standards No. 104-111, *Risk Assessment Standards*, issued by the American Institute of Certified Public Accountants' Auditing Standards Board (ASB), issue date March 2006.
4. Overview of Certified in Financial Forensics (CFF) credential, offered by the American Institute of Certified Public Accountants (AICPA) Business and Valuation Services (www.aicpa.org and http://fvs.aicpa.org/Memberships/Overview+of+Certified+in+Financial+Forensics+Credential.htm#press)

CHAPTER 8

The Importance of Internal Controls and Internal Audit

You are driving down a street in a familiar neighborhood. It is just after midnight, and there are no other cars on the road. As you approach a four-way stop sign, you note there are no headlights coming in any of the other directions. You have to decide whether to stop completely, slow down to a roll but otherwise keep going, or simply disregard the stop sign altogether, maintaining your speed. Most drivers will choose one of the first two options. However, if I added that the police have been clamping down on stop sign violators, especially during the midnight hours, due to an increase in drunk drivers, now most drivers would indicate they would stop completely. What changed? The higher risk of getting a ticket became a deterrent to running the stop sign.

In their most basic form, internal controls are nothing but a series of prescribed policies and procedures documenting how an organization authorizes, processes, and reports transactions. Designed properly, internal controls help ensure that transactions will be handled in an authorized, consistent, and compliant manner every time. However, simply identifying the processes or requirements will not ensure the effectiveness of the controls. The effectiveness of any internal control is based on three things: expectations, compliance, and consequences.

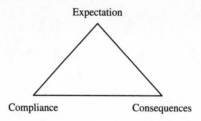

Take away any one corner of the triangle and the effectiveness is lost. Going back to the stop sign example, there is an expectation taught to every new driver that when the driver comes to an intersection with an octagonal red sign displaying the white letters "STOP," the driver will come to a complete stop and proceed through the intersection only after following other rules of driving. The consequence of getting a ticket or causing a serious accident is emphasized to all drivers to encourage compliance with stopping. However, everyone knows there are not enough police on the streets to watch every stop sign in existence. To ensure compliance and create a deterrent for running stop signs, police do in fact sit at random intersections and enforce the stop sign laws, demonstrating the genuine consequence of violating the law. However, if the police were ever to stop issuing tickets for running stop signs, without a doubt more drivers would simply ignore the signs altogether, increasing the odds of causing an accident.

Why Have Internal Controls?

If some level of guidelines and expectations are absent, potentially every individual transaction could be handled in a different fashion depending on the circumstances of each transaction—a free-for-all, if you will. Internal controls comprise a comprehensive set of documented policies and procedures designed to ensure that activity within an organization is authorized, approved, transacted, and reported in a prescribed, consistent, and conforming manner.

Often, the size and sophistication of an entity will dictate the level of internal controls and documentation in existence. As discussed in Chapter 7, under the requirements of the Sarbanes-Oxley Act (SOX), the management of any publicly traded entity is required to identify and assess the risk of fraudulent financial reporting within the entity's operations, as well as to assess the adequacy of their internal controls addressing the identified risks. The company, typically with the assistance of consultants who specialize in evaluating and implementing internal controls, is tasked to look for weaknesses and opportunities for fraud within the organization. Management cannot rely on the entity's external auditors to tell them what is required, as the design, implementation, and supervision of the control system is strictly management's responsibility. Only after management has assessed, designed, documented, and tested the internal controls can the external auditors independently assess and report on the internal controls and assessment made by management.

Given the overall size and level of sophistication of most publicly traded companies, an equally sophisticated and comprehensive system of internal controls would be expected in those organizations. But what about all the other organizations and entities that are not publicly traded and therefore not under the requirements of Sarbanes-Oxley?

The level of internal controls and documented policies and procedures will vary by individual entity, depending on the organization's size and resources. In many cases, little to no documentation exists beyond user notes, and the organization heavily depends on its outside auditors to identify shortfalls or design weaknesses as part of the annual financial statement audit.

As discussed in Chapter 7, new auditing standards enacted in 2007, echoing the sentiment of requirements under Sarbanes-Oxley, now require auditors to assess, document, and test each client's system of internal controls and accounting procedures, as well as assess the risk of fraud for each audit engagement.

The external auditors must report on the audited client's internal controls and determine how much reliance can be placed on each control for audit purposes.

Case Study 8.1 – Who Needs Internal Controls?

The owner of a client company called and asked me to meet with him to discuss a concern regarding his business. The company was a large construction contractor, with three related companies under common ownership. The main company was the number-one builder in the state and a preferred contractor on many public and private projects. The company had a chief financial officer and a well-staffed accounting department that used sophisticated construction software systems.

I went to the meeting on the scheduled day and was greeted by the owner. After a few minutes of small talk in the conference room, we were joined by the CFO. The owner described a substantial theft by a bookkeeper of another contractor, and wondered if something similar could occur within his entities. He stated he had a great handle on the construction side of things, knowing where each project was and how to determine whether things had gone south on a particular job. When it came to the financial transactions, however, he said he knew little to nothing about the controls and procedures that should be in place, let alone whether his companies had them or not. Since none of his companies required audited financial statements, his outside accountants provided him compilation-level financial statements along with his annual tax returns. He said his goal of the meeting was to determine the value and cost of having the company's internal controls and procedures objectively and independently evaluated.

At that point, the CFO chimed in and defended the controls and procedures he had implemented in each company. The CFO went on to state that having someone come into the companies with little to no knowledge of how each company operated would simply be a waste of money.

The owner disagreed, and I was hired to evaluate the controls and procedures of each company, starting with the smallest residential contractor. After spending two days with the bookkeeper dedicated to this company, I found that the accounting was completed on a separate system from the other entities. The bookkeeper provided me with the company's policies and procedures and then told me how transactions were really processed. Based on actual company practices versus documented procedures, the bookkeeper had sole responsibility for initiating, posting, and approving transactions, with little to no independent oversight except for a review of the monthly financial results.

The second company required a trip out of state to visit the actual location. I took pictures of the sad state of their inventory maintenance and discovered the signature stamp of the authorized signer on the desk of the controller. I learned that although the CFO reviewed and approved the financial reports of the company, much if not all of the financial decisions were made locally, without consent of the owner.

The last company I evaluated was the main company, and I found a higher level of accounting resources within their financial department. Consistent with the other companies, I found that documented policies and procedures existed in most areas. When I spoke with each staff member, however, I learned that the policies and procedures were rarely followed. In some cases, proper approvals were obtained, but in other cases transactions were recorded and processed without approval by the owner.

(Continued)

As a result of my visits and interviews, I documented my observations, along with practical recommendations to address each issue, in the form of three reports, one for each company. The smaller residential company received 12 pages of recommendations, and the middle company's report contained 20 pages. My report covering the largest company, which generated three times the combined revenue of the other two companies, contained 36 pages of recommendations. My recommendations ranged from simple things, such as segregating duties within cycles like cash receipts and cash disbursements, through more intense changes, such as the owner providing oversight and approval on transactions over set dollar thresholds.

The owner was appreciative and amazed at the number of issues identified during the project, and I earned the respect of the CFO, who had thought his systems and procedures were adequately designed and implemented.

Déjà Vu

Looking back, it appears the accounting profession has gone full circle, back to reliance upon an audit client's system of internal controls. Prior to my entry into the audit profession, I learned in college how to document, diagram, and evaluate an entity's controls and procedures. Flow charts and decision trees were commonly used to illustrate how each procedure flowed from start to end. Based on an assessment as to whether the control or procedure would accomplish the objective as well as prevent opportunities for error, the auditor would determine whether the control could be considered reliable or should be ignored altogether. If the control or procedure was not reliable, substantive audit procedures would be needed to accomplish the audit objectives and provide assurance not provided by the client's control.

When I started in public accounting, the documenting of client controls was quickly replaced with the substantive approach to auditing. Simply put, regardless of the level of internal controls in place within an audit client, we would assess the risk that the client's controls could not provide assurances at their maximum. This approach allowed us to ignore all of the client's controls, avoiding the documenting and testing we had previously performed, and we would perform audit procedures to substantiate the balances reported on the client's financial statements. Under this approach, we avoided interviewing the client staff and documenting the flows and processes, and we saved a significant amount of time and effort on our audits. The rationale was that all the material amounts reported were substantiated through independent audit procedures. Documenting a client's systems of internal controls became a lost art, practiced less and less outside of the large international accounting firms that mainly audited publicly traded companies.

Then 2001 rolled in with all the well-known audit failures. As a result, Sarbanes-Oxley was enacted. Several years later, many new auditing pronouncements no longer allow external auditors to simply ignore an audit client's internal controls. The new standards now require the auditors to document, assess, and test key internal controls and specifically report on their assessment and testing. The new standards no longer allow an auditing firm to discount a client's internal controls and rely solely on substantive procedures.

The enactment of Sarbanes-Oxley and other new auditing standards have created the need for audit firms to train their auditors in the lost art of documenting, assessing, and testing internal controls, something that at least the most recent generation of auditors may have never encountered since studying this area in college during their auditing classes.

Good Internal Controls

What exactly might good internal controls entail? Documented policies and procedures distributed to all employees for all employees to follow, as well as:

- Forms to standardize authorization of transactions and checklists to ensure all required steps are completed
- Segregation of key duties and responsibilities to ensure that no one individual or department can authorize, process, approve, record, and report transactions
- Independent approvals at appropriate levels based upon authorization thresholds
- Timely and accurate recording of the transactions in a manner that permits the preparation of financial statements and reports
- Regular independent reviews, performed by qualified individuals, of the financial information prepared and provided by management

These are certainly some of the measures that comprise good internal controls, but much more is required. Often a culture change is needed within an existing entity to discontinue past practices and adopt a more controlled environment. Management must start by setting the tone for the organization. Adopting a formal code of conduct and the commitment to make decisions and run the organization in an ethical manner will help establish an environment of compliance. Requiring every employee to comply with the organization's policies and procedures and supporting the culture of enforcing compliance to policies and procedures will help create that controlled environment.

Each process, then, needs to be objectively evaluated to ensure that it includes proper initiation, authorization, and approval. Checks and balances should be built into each process, along with the requirement to reconcile the activity on a regular basis.

Next, management must educate and train the employees, provide them with the documented policies and procedures, and emphasize the importance of complying with all policies and procedures. Management must also support supervisors and managers when noncompliance is identified, and reinforce the importance of compliance to the offending individuals. To ensure compliance, management must include in the documentation the potential consequences to individuals for noncompliance.

Once communicated and fully implemented, the transactions need to be monitored and reviewed to ensure compliance with the policies and procedures. Feedback loops should be designed and implemented to allow communication of noncompliance back to the individual or the individual's supervisor to be addressed. Repeated patterns of noncompliance should result in consequences, up through termination of employment.

Throughout the period under review or scrutiny, individual transactions populate the systems, culminating in the accumulation of all transactions within the various ledgers and journals of the accounting system. Controls and procedures are needed to ensure the timely reconciliation and review of the subsystems, control balances, ledgers, and journals. Once key account balances are reconciled, financial reports should be drafted, reviewed, and scrutinized prior to distribution to end users. Individuals responsible for preparing the financial reports should be required to provide supporting workpapers and reconciliations evidencing the completeness and accuracy of the financial reports.

Lastly, the control environment does not stop with senior management. The board of directors of any organization, along with audit and finance committees, serves as a critical control measure over the financial integrity of its entity. Many boards have become sophisticated in response to their responsibility for ensuring the financial stability of the organization along with their increased personal risk, should something go wrong and go undetected.

The audit committee's role must include monitoring senior management activity, reviewing the effectiveness of internal controls, overseeing the internal audit function (if one exists), and reviewing the financial reports on a regular basis. The audit committee must also review management's performance and the company's code of conduct at least annually. It is one thing to have a code of conduct, but it is another to review it regularly and enforce it.

Many companies have struggled to develop a good control environment and system of internal controls. With the passage of SOX and the new auditing standards, management will now be under the watchful eye of more independent boards and external auditors and will be held directly accountable for the company's financial statements.

Internal Audit

Just as the assessment of internal controls by external auditors has gone full circle, so has the importance of internal auditors. Over the past 20 or more years, the role of the internal auditor has been eliminated in all but the largest organizations. Viewed as overhead and nonessential, internal audit positions were often the first to be eliminated during cost savings measures.

After the accounting failures of 2001 and the passage of Sarbanes-Oxley, companies scrambled to recruit qualified individuals to fulfill internal audit or SOX-related positions. The problem many organizations faced was that experienced internal auditors had left the field after the jobs dried up, and most students had stopped pursuing internal audit careers because there were few opportunities in that field.

An effective internal audit function, with adequate staff to carry it out, is an essential part of any internal control system. The internal audit team should have the full support of senior management, the board of directors, and the audit committee to perform their procedures and report their findings. Internal auditors are integral to the effectiveness of the internal controls by going into the field and testing transactions to ensure policies and procedures are followed.

Even smaller entities with little to no means to justify a dedicated internal audit position should draw upon existing resources within the accounting and finance areas to perform periodic audits and procedures that ensure compliance with policies and procedures. Having a staff accountant go out into the field to visit a site and perform a surprise test count or reconciliation creates a deterrent, as well as a means for detecting a potential problem. Unfortunately, many smaller organizations never consider the importance of these measures and, coupled with lean accounting departments running beyond capacity, these procedures are never even considered, let alone performed. The end result is the belated discovery of fraudulent activity that could have and should have been detected months if not years earlier, minimizing the financial loss to the organization.

Case Study 8.2 – Best of Intentions?

Life Skills, a local nonprofit mental health organization specializing in providing community residential living arrangements to individuals with diminished capabilities, had a main campus and eight community homes. Funding for the program was obtained through federal and state disability payments to the residents, as well as through a few small grants.

(Continued)

153

Five to eight residents lived within each home, with transportation and other services provided by the organization.

Administration was located in Life Skills' main building, along with development, finance, IT, and a few of the entity's other social programs. A resident manager who reported directly to the Director of Program Service was responsible for each home.

The organization had designed and documented policies and procedures to ensure all programs were properly run and tracked and were compliant with federal, state, and granting agency guidelines. The finance department consisted of a finance director, senior accountant, and two accounting staff members, who focused on billing and accounts payable.

Individuals from administration and accounting rarely, if ever, visited the eight homes. Each resident manager came into the accounting department weekly to approve invoices, submit his or her employees' timecards, and review any issues with the programs. In addition to managing the house and services provided to residents, each resident manager was responsible for maintaining the bank accounts and funds of each resident, along with a petty cash account.

The organization received each resident's federal and/or state check directly. Acting as the resident's payer representative, the organization calculated what each resident could afford to pay for rent and administration, based upon stipulated guidelines. Any residual funds were paid by check to each resident for personal spending. A passbook checking account was required to be established for each resident, and it was the resident manager's responsibility to bring each resident to the bank to complete the banking. As funds were requested or spent by the residents, each transaction was required to be logged on the resident's banking logs, and store receipts were required for every purchase. Each resident's activity was required to be maintained in a separate and secure folder to enable the reconciliation of each resident's funds.

Based on the recommendations of the organization's outside auditors, the organization decided to perform some spot checks and surprise visits to individual homes. The senior accountant checked with the director of program services to determine whether resident managers would be at their homes on select days but didn't mention anything about going out to visit the resident managers.

The first visit went as expected. Resident files and funds were maintained as required, and the petty cash was balanced and reconciled. Similar experiences were encountered at the second and third home visited.

When the senior accountant arrived at the fourth home, the one furthest away and located in a remote section of town, she was greeted by the resident manager and her assistant. The senior accountant instructed the resident manager, who was unaware of the purpose of the visit, to retrieve the resident files, as well as the petty cash fund. A few minutes later the resident manager returned with an accordion file containing the resident files, along with a manila folder containing a few receipts.

After reviewing the petty cash activity, the senior accountant reviewed the file containing the resident files and funds. Noting that there were no separate files or bank accounts in the folder for each resident, the senior accountant asked the resident manager for those records. The resident manager stated there were no other records, and that ledgers and passbook accounts had not been maintained. When asked where the funds were for each resident, the site manager

(Continued)

stated the funds were in her personal bank account. She explained that when each resident's check was received, she had to bring each resident to the bank clear across town. However, right around the corner from the home was a local branch, where the resident manager maintained her personal accounts. In the spirit of minimizing the time away from the home, she had deposited the resident's checks into her personal checking account each month, and whenever a resident needed cash, she would withdraw funds via the branch ATM. The resident manager rationalized that the resident's funds were more secure in her account than maintained at the home, and were only an ATM withdrawal away whenever they needed money.

The senior accountant asked the resident manager for any logs, ledgers or other records used to track each resident's funds, along with the supporting receipts. The resident manager stated she never kept any records beyond her bank statements and never retained any receipts to show how the funds were used, because much of their expenses were paid in cash.

Needless to say, the senior accountant told the resident manager that commingling the resident's funds with her personal checking account was inappropriate, and that the lack of records and receipts would make it impossible to objectively determine how all the funds had been used. Beyond inappropriate, her actions were also in direct violation of documented policies and procedures for managing resident funds.

The senior accountant reported her findings to the director of finance as well as the director of program services. Their response was to remove the resident manager from the home and commence an investigation into her banking activity. Bank statements were obtained for the resident manager's bank account, and the deposits containing the resident's funds were identified. However, as the resident manager had indicated, much of the fund activity had been completed via ATM withdrawals. Absent records to reconstruct the activity, the organization was never able to determine whether all the resident funds had been used for the benefit of the residents. The resident manager was terminated for failing to comply with policies and procedures. A few months later, the organization learned that the same resident manager was working for a similar organization.

The initial organization had no idea that the resident manager was commingling resident funds and likely diverting their funds for personal use until the senior accountant performed a surprise audit. Had the finance department not initiated the visits to each home, the resident manager would have continued to use resident funds, and a larger financial loss could have resulted at her hands.

The first several chapters defined fraud, explained different types of fraud, provided insight on why it has been occurring at an alarming rate, and detailed many specific fraud schemes. In Chapters 7 and 8, we discussed general responses to fraud, including new regulations and requirements, as well as measures that organizations can implement through internal controls and internal auditing to prevent and detect instances of financial fraud. The focus up to this point has, as previous author Howard Davia referred to it, been "proactive fraud investigation," hoping to stem the growing trend.

Now it is time to examine the issues surrounding potential investigative issues in response to the detection of fraudulent activity. The remaining chapters focus on reacting to an allegation or actual instance of fraud, or what Davia termed "reactive fraud investigation."

CHAPTER 9

Evidence

Evidence is crucial to a successful investigation. The search for evidence to prove fraud is the essence of an investigation. For most investigations where fraud has occurred, or at least where fraud is strongly suspected, collecting sufficient evidence to ensure a successful claim or conviction for fraud is usually the deciding factor on whether to proceed. Unfortunately, many people who are not adequately trained in fraud investigations fail to understand the vital importance of evidence. Prosecution on the cases they develop often is declined, even though they are confident of their findings and may, in fact, be correct. Evidence transcends the gap between the investigators' firsthand knowledge of case circumstances and what is conveyed to a judge or jury.

Many auditors and investigators tend to develop the consequences of fraud, such as the amount and duration of the theft. However, when it comes to identifying the individuals involved in the fraud scheme, they fall short unless they have at least rudimentary training in the nature of evidence. Good investigators must ask the following questions: Is there additional evidence to be detected, and are the investigators sufficiently trained, experienced, and skilled to identify and detect it? Undoubtedly, this accounts for the failure of discovered fraud cases to advance to a stage where they are fully documented and prepared for prosecution.

Many fraud perpetrators are very clever and leave few, if any, clues to detect and unravel their scheme. In these instances, the most experienced investigators are challenged to detect recognizable evidence of their fraud scheme. However, the vast majority are not experienced or trained in fraud detection and investigative techniques and do not possess a sufficient level of knowledge of the evidence required to pursue a case. As a result, many fraud cases do not get prosecuted and may go unresolved.

It is incumbent upon anyone who will potentially perform fraud investigations to get the requisite training and experience available regarding evidence and all the other important issues related to fraud investigations. Refer to Chapter 7 for a discussion on the organizations such as the Association of Certified Fraud Examiners (ACFE) who provide such training.

What Is Evidence?

So what is evidence? According to *Black's Law Dictionary*, evidence is "something (including testimony, documents and tangible objects) that tends to prove or disprove the existence of an alleged fact."[1] When it comes to financial investigations, evidence can be obtained from many sources and in different forms. Evidence can be in the form of verbal information, such as facts and details provided during an interview, or in documentation form. In fraud-related matters of any type, reports, statement, ledgers, checks, invoices, receipts, and other documents are a common source of evidence.

Evidence can also be provided electronically as images or files originating from an individual's laptop or computer hard drive, or as programs and data maintained on a company's file servers. The electronic information may be stored locally on the business's network, on a server in the next state or another country, or it could be stored on a third-party server accessed and maintained via the Internet. Many business phone systems run on a computerized system with dedicated computers, allowing discovery of phone logs and retrieval of electronically saved voice messages. E-mails, contacts, calendar entries, and other electronic information may even be preserved as evidence from personal handheld devices, including BlackBerries and cell phones.

When it comes to identifying sources of evidence, the experienced investigator will have to think intuitively and creatively to identify every possible source of information.

Case Study 9.1 – Creative Tracking

Unauthorized transactions were identified in a local medical practice's billing system. The entries were isolated within the system; they had been made early in the morning or late in the day after business hours. The entries were traced to patient files and payment remittances, and it was determined that the transactions were used to conceal insurance collection payments diverted from the practice. The practice had no security measures or monitoring systems in place within the office to determine who was present when the changes were made.

After reviewing employee time and earning records, billing system transaction journals, telephone logs, and written information within patient records, the universe of possible perpetrators narrowed to a few employees. Further procedures, including interviews with each employee seemed to point towards one individual who had both the access and the knowledge to make the changes. However, nothing existed within the practice to definitively show that the individual was present when the changes were posted.

(Continued)

Then the investigator thought about other possible sources of information available to resolve the matter. He remembered that the prime suspect parked her car in a controlled parking garage adjacent to the building, and that she had been issued a numbered parking access card that she used to enter and exit the garage each day. In an attempt to show that the suspect was at the building on the dates and times of the changes, the investigator obtained a copy of the garage access log from the parking management company's system, in both electronic and printed forms. The electronic log was then searched for entries specific to the suspect's card number, and only those transactions were extracted from the file. The result showed that the suspect's car was parked in the garage on the dates and times when changes were made to the system. The investigator thought if the suspect's car was at the building, it was likely the suspect was in the office during the times in question.

Confronted with the parking lot information, transaction logs, and patient files, the suspect resigned her employment from the practice, signed a release, and through her attorney repaid the practice the total amount determined to be diverted by her from the practice along with the costs of the investigation.

Training and experience are required to properly identify, collect, preserve, and maintain evidence in a manner that will ensure it will be admissible into court, if needed, after the investigation has been concluded. Proper evidence management includes taking physical possession of identified items, carefully making copies if needed for investigative purposes, documenting the source and description of each item, and preserving the original items in the state and condition they were found to ensure no changes were possible from the time each item was collected until the time each item will be offered in court as evidence in the case.

Simply collecting and protecting potential evidence will not be enough to ensure the admissibility of the identified items. The person who collected the items must be able to identify each and every step taken with each item of potential evidence, from the time each item was collected until the time it was offered as evidence in the case. Measures need to be implemented to ensure that as few individuals as possible have access to the evidence, and logs need to be maintained to identify who had access to the evidence, as well as to document all movement of each item. Therefore, it behooves the investigator to copy and preserve the items as quickly as possible after collection to minimize the need to access and re-access the items and to reduce the number of entries required to track the activity and movement. Two copies will allow a working copy and a copy that can be used to make additional copies. Work can be performed using the copies, with the original evidence remaining secured as evidence.

Documentation

Documentation cannot be overemphasized when it comes to evidence and investigating fraud. In my investigations, I use spiral-bound steno pads and carry evidence labels for collecting items that later may be deemed evidence supporting my investigation. In addition to documenting the procedures I performed, items I collected, and specific location of each item, I often supplement my notes with a sketch of the areas where the evidence was collected. I have been asked in more than one instance to describe in as much detail as possible the exact location of a particular item. Questions I have been asked include how many chairs were in the room, whether the drawer was open or closed, and whether there was anything else on the desk. Often, these questions are raised months, if not years, after the items were collected. My sketches, often primitive rough drawings of the rooms or areas searched, have proven invaluable in helping me recall the details needed.

In addition to a notebook, an investigator may find the use of a handheld audio recorder, commonly referred to as a dictaphone, to be extremely handy when collecting evidence or conducting interviews. Besides having to carry around a pad and pen, in some instances there may not be sufficient time to enable written documentation of each and every step completed. Using a dictaphone to record all the critical information in rich detail as it occurs will enable someone to transcribe the activity later into the documentation for the files. The tapes themselves can be preserved as well, to be replayed if needed.

Consider taking pictures or video-recordings of the areas, especially in today's electronic age in which cameras and video recorders are included as features on most cell phones. I have photographed areas before and after a search, as well as photographed items still in their original place before they were collected into evidence. In the cases of covert investigations conducted during the middle of the night so as to not alert targeted employees to our presence, we have used photographs taken before and after our procedures to ensure the areas were left exactly as we found them. Digital cameras will work for these missions, but we have found that Polaroids work even better, because you can lay out all the pictures and compare them to the way things were left, versus having to view one picture at a time on the small display on the digital camera.

When shopping for the most practical tools to use when collecting evidence, consider the evidentiary issues you will need to prove to ensure the admissibility of the evidence. Spiral-bound steno pads that identify the number of pages right on the covers ensure that all the pages of notes have been preserved and provided if requested. Purchasing a dictaphone that uses removable tapes versus digital memory means that the tapes for each investigation can be preserved if needed, rather than buying a new dictaphone for each investigation. Using pre-numbered forms, labels, and other items will allow for tracking and accounting for all items collected.

Equally important to the tools used to preserve evidence is the establishment of a routine or procedure that is followed consistently with every investigation. Documenting the process and adhering to a standard methodology will best ensure that every step or measure will be completed each time an investigation is conducted. Standardization and documentation are even more important when multiple individuals are involved with conducting investigations, to ensure that each investigator follows the same protocols and that every investigation is completed in a consistent and expected manner.

Regarding electronic evidence, the sources available to capture electronically stored information change almost daily, with new access to valuable electronic data created with every new gadget offered on the market. While many accountants and investigators possess sufficient computer competence to copy electronic information, undelete files and e-mails, or even capture an image from a hard drive, employing a specialist in computer forensics is highly recommended, especially in high-profile or high-stakes cases. The specialist will have specific experience in capturing, verifying, and maintaining the electronic information, will have better tools and software to recover lost or deleted information, and will be best suited to testify regarding how the electronic evidence was obtained and preserved, should that be needed in the case.

The success of an investigation depends greatly on the existence and strength of the evidence available. Even with positive proof that fraudulent activity did in fact occur, the reality is that without sufficient information and evidence available to investigate the fraud, there may be no point in wasting efforts and funds to pursue the matter. Even if a conclusion could be reached at the end of the investigation, law enforcement or the prosecutor could decline to pursue the case if sufficient credible evidence is not available, or if the evidence has not been properly collected and preserved.

Simply bringing collected evidence back to the office and leaving it in a file cabinet drawer or audit bag will not suffice for proper control to ensure the chain of evidence. Collecting evidence at a client location, locking it in the car, and stopping for supper or an errand after leaving the client may constitute a break in the chain and jeopardize the evidence. Measures must be taken to ensure all the original evidence collected was immediately secured, with access restricted to authorized individuals. Ideally, collected evidence should be brought directly from the collection point to the office, logged in, and secured before ending the process or performing any other procedures.

In some cases, too much time may have lapsed, certain requested information may no longer exist or be available, or there could be other reasons that access to critical information is prevented. It is common for evidence to have been destroyed, accidentally or intentionally, or for an opposing party to quite simply decide they won't provide any information to support the investigation. Fires, floods, physical moves, and box mislabeling can all occur and will prevent access to the original information. While it is optimal to support every investigation with original evidence, typically, all is not lost when the original evidence cannot or will not be provided. The investigation can continue, based upon the "best evidence" or "best information available" rule.

Is a cancelled check received from a bank along with the monthly statement considered evidence? What about the bank-provided image of a cancelled check? How about when a company generates and mails a check to a vendor, and the vendor electronically converts the check into an electronic payment and then shreds the original check received from the company. What is considered evidence in that situation?

What about a draft of a financial statement, found on a controller's hard drive, that reflects amounts that are different from the final issued version of the financial statements? What about the e-mails and memos sent between the main office and a branch location discussing the need to move inventory out of a warehouse prior to the auditor's arrival? Are the drafts, e-mails, and memos considered evidence? The answer to all of these questions depends on what and how the evidence will be used to support or refute an issue.

A good rule of thumb when conducting a financial investigation is to collect and preserve any potential evidence once it is identified. If the items have been collected and preserved in a timely manner, the only risk with this approach is that more evidence than needed will be collected and maintained. Later in the investigation, the preserved items can be reviewed, and any items deemed not relevant or needed can simply be returned. The alternative is to collect only those items deemed pertinent during the investigation, at the risk of later learning that the additional items not collected are needed but are no longer available.

In the words of the authors of previous editions of *Fraud 101*, evidence is the heart of a fraud investigation. Find as much of it as possible, preserve it, corroborate it, and document, document, document!

Case Study 9.2 – Equipment Repair: Contractor's False Claims

The contract was a time and materials contract—that is, it provided that the contractor would be reimbursed on the basis of the number of direct labor hours he expended

(Continued)

on equipment repaired at a predetermined hourly rate, as specified in the contract. The contractor would also be reimbursed for the actual cost of repair parts purchased. The set hourly rate had been bid on by the contractor in competition against other contractors, and it included his average direct labor cost per hour, along with prorated overhead and administrative costs and an approved profit.

The contract also required that the contractor make his records available for audit, should it be requested. An audit disclosed that the contractor had falsely inflated the labor hours claimed to have been expended and had falsely claimed the purchase of repair parts. Through validating the authenticity of suppliers, the auditors found many of the parts suppliers had addresses that turned out to be vacant lots.

Through an audit of the contractor's payroll record, it was determined the hours charged to jobs of individual employees' time for allegedly working on jobs far exceeded the total weekly hours that the employees had worked and been paid.

Armed with seemingly indisputable evidence of fraud, the auditor prepared a report supported with the evidence collected, and the contractor was indicted, prosecuted, and convicted of fraud in federal court. Subsequent to the verdict, the assistant U.S. attorney who prosecuted the case complained to the auditors that he had difficulty convincing the jury of the contractor's guilt and had come close to failing. The prosecutor told the auditors to bring stronger evidence in the future to show the contractor's "intent" to defraud the government. The prosecutor was looking for evidence that the contractor had committed fraud on more than this one contract, thereby making it clear that he had fraudulent intent and a clear pattern to defraud the government.

In this case, the auditors believed there was compelling evidence of the contractor's culpability. However, the contractor's defense attorney had raised a question as to whether the contractor's actions rose to the level of criminal, rationalizing that if there was no other evidence of any other potentially criminal conduct, perhaps the contractor's actions were attributable to careless bookkeeping or a series of mistakes and errors.

Interestingly, the same contractor's guilt later appeared to be certain in the context of a related case, which involved a U.S. Air Force sergeant who was allegedly in collusion with the contractor. The sergeant was tried separately by a military court for sending perfectly serviceable generators, not in need of repair, to the contractor, who merely stored them for a short time before returning them and billing the government for work not performed. According to the sergeant, the proceeds were split with the contractor.

Having sufficient evidence to support the results of an investigation, coupled with maintaining the correct level of documentation regarding the collected evidence and investigative measures performed, cannot be overemphasized and will have a direct impact on successful achievement of the desired resolution of the matter. To ensure both will occur, conscious thought and advanced planning are required. Drawing upon my experience working on an ambulance as an EMT, we train and plan for medical calls of every nature, even ones we know that we will likely never receive. The equipment and supplies needed are stocked and checked daily, and our protocols for completing calls are documented and provided to us frequently to ensure every call is handled consistently. In the context of any investigation, it is best to assemble the required supplies and items needed and document the investigative process in advance to ensure readiness for when the call is received.

In the next chapter, we discuss issues relating to the actual investigative process, identify three types of fraud-related investigations, and discuss strategy or approach considerations when conducting an investigation, should an investigation be warranted.

Note

1. Garner, Bryan A. (ed.-in-chief), *Black's Law Dictionary* 8th edition (West, a Thomson Business: 2004).

CHAPTER 10

Conducting Fraud Investigations: A Practical Approach

B ased upon my personal experience, I have found that fraud investigations fall into three general categories: proactive investigations (no fraud is suspected); discovery investigations (suspected fraudulent or unexplained activity); and supportive investigations (fraud is known to have occurred). Some of the procedures typically performed in each of these categories are similar in nature, but the strategy and approach employed on each type should be very different.

Proactive Fraud Investigations

Proactive procedures may be conducted to identify, measure, and/or test compliance with established policies, procedures, or internal controls. For example, a medical practice with five locations had documented procedures regarding the collection of patient payments at the time of their office visit. The procedures called for the completion of a three-part receipt for every payment received; the white copy was to be provided to the patient. A surprise visit to any of the locations to review a period's worth of transactions could be performed, tracing every patient payment during the period back to the receipt book on hand. This measure would indicate whether the employees were in fact following protocol by issuing receipts or not. The periodic audit of the receipting expectation would also send a clear message to the employees regarding the practice's attitude toward controls and the importance of that particular procedure.

Procedures can also be performed proactively within high fraud-risk areas, or areas susceptible to fraudulent activity, even when no fraud indicators are present. For example, employees have been defrauding their employers through travel and entertainment reimbursement for as long as employers have been reimbursing employees for such expenses. Although measures should be in place to ensure that proper receipts were submitted, along with a supervisor's approval in order for a reimbursement check to be issued, the legitimacy of the supporting receipts may not have been verified or scrutinized by someone experienced in fraudulent receipt submission. An independent and objective review of the supporting receipts on selected employee reimbursements could measure employees' compliance to the receipts requirement as well as the accounts payable department's compliance with the rules regarding supporting receipts and supervisor approvals.

In conducting such a review, the first question to answer is whether all the supporting receipts were provided. Secondly, one would look to ensure the required supervisor approval was obtained. Lastly, the reviewer would critically review each expense item to determine whether each appeared to be business-related and reasonable.

Discovery Investigations

Often an investigation is initiated based on an educated hunch or a belief that something might be wrong within the company or organization. It might be related to an employee's behavior, or the fact that inventory shortages continued to occur even after the implementation of tighter physical controls and cycle counts, or even by the simple fact that a company or a division has been experiencing unprecedented growth in sales or revenues, along with cost reductions, without a corresponding increase in cash flows.

Whatever the sign or symptom, an investigation needs to be initiated to determine the underlying cause and identify what happened or is happening. Discovery investigations may even result from proactive investigations.

Take the medical practice example discussed above. An audit was conducted to determine compliance with providing payment receipts should be initiated. During the audit, it was learned that each time a patient pays his or her co-payment in cash, a receipt was provided. In tracing the payment to the patient's account on the billing system, no corresponding payment entry was reflected. However, an adjustment entry was posted to the patient's account for the cash amount on the same day the payment was received. The proactive procedures initiated to ensure compliance identified the signs of an actual employee theft scheme occurring in that location.

Using the inventory example, a few different things could be occurring to cause the differences. The most obvious explanation would be that someone with access to the inventory was stealing it. But what if proper procedures were never implemented to remove items from stock or to restock returned items? Could it be possible that the inventory system used mishandled these transactions, causing the differences? The answer is: Anything is possible.

Case Study 10.1 – Employee Theft or Free Stuff?

A regional retailer of outdoor recreational items had an issue with the reliability of their inventory counts within

(Continued)

their central warehouse and their more than 30 locations. Periodic physical counts of inventory in each location compared to reported inventory levels of selected items revealed consistent differences, even after the implementation of a new inventory tracking system. The most frequent differences were with smaller products, or accessories, which were typically sold to complement the larger ticket items. Employees were paid a small base salary, with most of their compensation earned through commissions on their sales. Management was certain employees were stealing the accessory items due to their size and ease of theft, and selling them at bargain prices to customers for cash. The employees would then pocket the cash, supplementing their legitimate earnings.

After observing customer transactions (unbeknownst to the employees) and conducting interviews with employees at the retail locations, we identified the true underlying cause of the differences. When the larger ticket items were sold, if the customer purchased the accessory items as part of a "bundle" at the time of the sale, the sale would be rung up under the bundle code, and the individual stock items comprising the bundle would not be rung up through the register. The accessory items in question were always included in bundle deals.

After tracing sales transactions for both individual accessory items as well as bundle sales through the underlying systems, it was determined that the issue resided within the point of sale system. When the point of sale system was implemented, product items (or SKUs) were established in the system. The register system was then integrated to the new inventory system. The individual stock items and the bundle deals were created as separate transaction items.

The individual items were entered with their associated cost and suggested retail price. However, the bundled items were entered as a unique item, with summarized costs and prices of all the included items. Herein lay the issue causing the differences. The bundled items were never configured under the sales code (or SKU) to relieve all of the accessory items from inventory. Therefore, every time a bundled sale occurred, all of the accessory items were physically provided to the customer as they should have been, reducing the store's physical inventory, but the store's electronic inventory records were never relieved for all of the accessory items.

It was also learned that certain employees created their own unauthorized bundle deals with customers, to make their sales and accordingly make their commissions on those sales, by simply throwing in whatever accessory items were needed to close the deal. This development complicated any calculation of inventory differences to determine how much was attributable to the system configuration versus employee theft to generate commissions.

It is critical to remain objective as well as skeptical in performing procedures in any investigation. Fraud is one common explanation for unusual or unexplained activity, but it is not the only explanation.

Supportive Investigations

Fraud has occurred, or is strongly believed to have occurred. The financial statements have been found to contain false or misleading information, or to omit material matters that have a significant impact on the results and balances. Customer payments have been diverted by someone in finance, the purchasing agent has been receiving kickbacks from a vendor, or highly marketable inventory items have been stolen from stock. The specifics of the scheme may or may not be known. However, it is more than a hunch that fraudulent activity has occurred and may be continuing to occur.

The objective of these types of investigations is to determine what, who, how, when, how long, how much, why, and other underlying details of the issue. The goal of supportive investigations is to obtain sufficient credible evidence to support the underlying conclusions, which in turn will be used to provide recourse for the victim company or organization. It is important not only to prove what actually occurred, but also prove that no other explanations could be possible.

Case Study 10.2 – A Small Difference in a Bank Reconciliation

A local nonprofit organization called to report a small reconciling difference within a designated bank account. The director was adamant that his prior accountant, a CPA who worked within the organization for several years and was responsible for all the bank accounts, had stolen funds from the organization. During the initial meeting with the director, a capital improvements account with a reconciled difference of $500,000 ("small reconciling difference") was identified. Throughout the meeting, the director ranted and raved over the accountant's behavior and his desire to have her both arrested and disbarred from the CPA profession.

During a meeting with the former accountant's coworkers at the organization, it was learned the director and the accountant had never liked each other, and the director was happy to see her leave. The staff also described how the organization had experienced their worst financial year in recent history. A review of the prior year's funding of the organization revealed that advances from a significant endowment fund had been received in past years to supplement operating cash requirements. Further, it was identified that during the current year, funds had started to come into the organization to support a new capital campaign. Upon reviewing the activity, no endowment funding was found for the current year—their worst financial year—and yet the organization met all their operating cost requirements. How could that have happened?

The capital funds received, rather than being segregated into a separate account, had been commingled into the operating account and subsequently used to fund operating costs. Once quantified, the organization simply needed to make a transfer from the endowments into the capital campaign account, rectifying the bookkeeping differences. Reasonable explanation—absolutely. Did the accountant steal any money? Not a dime. Thankfully, the director refrained from initiating a defamation campaign against the former accountant, or he and the organization would have defended rightful litigation.

The results of a supportive investigation, typically provided in the form of a report, will likely be used to remedy the matter, whether to support criminal charges or to identify prospective changes that should be implemented with internal controls or financial procedures. How the investigation was conducted, how evidence was collected and preserved, and how the report was written will be subject to significant scrutiny.

Strategy

Many professionals who are unqualified or inexperienced in fraud will encounter an opportunity to aid a client or friend with a potential fraud-related matter. My experience has shown that untrained individuals, driven by the *CSI* effect and the potential to earn significant fees, drive straight out to the client's location and jump right into performing procedures. Typically, they begin by searching through personal computers, laptops, work-stations, and server hard drives, looking for electronic records and relevant e-mails. They shuffle and sift through volumes of financial records, bank statements, paid invoices, payroll details, and petty cash support. After much effort, at a high cost to the client, they may or may not identify critical evidence support-ing or refuting the allegations. The result typically ends with the client being no further along in resolving a potential fraud issue and likely having spent a significant amount of funds on professional fees. Worse yet for the client, the inexperi-enced professionals probably did not follow proper investigative and evidence preservation techniques, potentially invalidating anything they may have found and preventing anyone hired sub-sequently from adequately investigating the issue. The helpful offer turns into a nightmare for the client or friend.

Beyond the investigator's inexperience with fraud, why did the investigation not attain the goals and objectives identified within the strategy-setting session? The answer is common and basic—they never had an initial strategy or goal-setting discus-sion with the client, client's counsel, and others pertinent to the matter prior to initiating any investigative procedures. An initial meeting or discussion would have provided, at a minimum, the purpose of the engagement, the goals and objectives, and the potential remedies available if fraud was identified. The initial meeting would have also ensured that all parties involved were in agreement with and had an understanding of the approach to be used. Without such pre-procedure planning, the strategy typically used is a "needle in the haystack" approach.

Case Study 10.3 – The Blur

To illustrate the importance of initial planning, here is an analogy from a hazy period in my life. When our first son was born, he didn't sleep more than 45 minutes at a time for his first 10 months—a very long period I often refer to as "the blur." My wife and I were so tired all the time from having interrupted sleep every day and night for ten months that I don't remember much of it in deep detail. I do remember setting out at times to run errands or to pick things up at the store. I can remember several early trips during which, hours after I left, my wife would call looking for me. I would tell her where I was, and that I couldn't remember why I was there. Each time I set out for one destination she found me in a completely different store, at times in a distant town. After I had been rescued from being lost on several occasions, my wife put a new strategy in place before sending me out anywhere. She and I would discuss briefly where I was supposed to be going and what I was to be doing before each trip. Then she would write out the plan, so I could take the note with me on my journey. Lo and behold, once we implemented this approach I managed to hit all the right stores and return with only the things I was supposed to buy, and I never found myself wondering aimlessly around a Walmart in some distant town. Having our initial planning meeting coupled with a written plan kept me from appearing on the side of a milk carton.

I cannot emphasize enough the importance of having an initial strategy-setting meeting with as many stakeholders present as possible before initiating any procedures on any type of investigation.

Predication

First and foremost, a discussion must be held regarding the facts and circumstances leading to the potential need for the investigation. Proper constitutional criminal investigations are required to be conducted based upon probable cause. Probable cause, as defined in *Black's Law Dictionary*, is "a reasonable ground to suspect that a person has committed or is committing a crime or that a place contains specific items connected to a crime. Probable cause amounts to more than a bare suspicion but less than evidence that would justify a conviction."[1] This high standard of investigative behavior traces its roots directly to the Fourth Amendment of the Constitution.

Fraud investigations are no different and often involve criminal investigation, especially when evidence is known to exist proving that fraud did, in fact, occur. However, in proactive and discovery investigations, fraudulent activity is not known to have occurred. Therefore, these types of fraud investigations need to be based upon and supported by *predication*—the basis or reason for initiating an investigation. The predication could be proactive or reactive; it could even be random, if proactive investigations are commonly performed as a result of random selection to ensure compliance, for example.

Predication is similar to probable cause, but to a lesser degree. It is a reasonable basis for initiating and conducting an investigation. In resolving claims raised by the targets of an investigation, an independent and objective party, such as a mediator, could review the reason the investigation was initiated to determine whether there was sufficient basis at that time to move forward with an investigation. Without predication, the investigator and the sponsoring company or organization are very much at risk to defend claims for, among other things, harassment, defamation, and malicious prosecution, especially if the investigation results in no findings of fraudulent activity.

The Investigative Plan

Based on a successful initial meeting and the determination of predication, the next step would be to identify how the goals and objectives will be accomplished. What specific steps and procedures will be performed, and in what order, to carry out the investigation? Who will need to be interviewed, and what information will be solicited from each interviewee? What records will be needed, and for what period of time? Will the records be obtained in hard copy or in an electronic format? What will we do with the documents or files once we are provided with the information? How will they be referenced, and where will they be stored? Will a computer expert be needed to preserve electronic evidence?

These considerations are some of the specific steps and measures that need to be contemplated and written out in the form of an investigative plan or audit program prior to initiating the first procedure. The written plan is important to the success of the investigation for two reasons. First, as steps and procedures are identified and written, other measures will be identified, leading to more thought about how the investigation should be conducted and the order in which the procedures should be performed. Second, the written plan acts as a reminder of all the procedures that need to be completed to ensure a complete and thorough investigation. Often, once investigative measures have been initiated, interviews have begun, documents have been produced, and pieces of the puzzle have been identified, important contemplated procedures can be overlooked or missed. In some cases, if certain procedures are not performed in a timely manner, events could occur that prevent the steps from ever being performed.

Case Study 10.4 – Take Two Aspirin and Call Me

A physician in a small practice suspected patient payments were being stolen by the practice's bookkeeper. Rather than call someone experienced in these matters, the physician started his own investigation. After reviewing the receipt books and patient files, he discovered differences between the payments. He obtained the password to gain access to the practice's accounting system from the bookkeeper, and unknowingly alerted the bookkeeper that he was on to her scheme. Within the system, he found yet more differences between the receipt books and the recorded deposits into the bank account. He ended their day by asking the bookkeeper about some of the differences and was provided explanations for each of them.

The office was closed for the next week, as the physician was on a planned vacation in warmer climates. The first morning back, when the physician came to the office, he noticed forced entry marks around the door lock. Once inside he realized the receipt books were not on his desk where he had left them. He asked the staff if anyone had been in the office and moved them—no one claimed to have come into the office during the week. When they turned on the computer, the hard drive would not boot up. Even after computer specialists were called to help, the computer never started again.

The bookkeeper reported to work as usual and acted as surprised as everyone else in the office. Later in the day, the physician determined that patient files were missing from the shelves, including the ones he had reviewed before his vacation. The police were called, fingerprints were collected on the door, and the staff were interviewed, especially the bookkeeper. No arrest was ever made for the "burglary," none of the records were ever located, and the computer was replaced with a new one. Luckily, the patient scheduling and billing system had been backed up shortly before the incident, but only those files were included in the backup. There was no backup for the accounting system, and a new system was implemented from scratch. How long had the embezzlement gone on, and how much was stolen? The physician will never know.

Could this have been prevented? Could the investigation been handled differently? If the physician had thought about what information he would need to determine whether fraudulent activity existed, identified the steps and measures he would need to take to preserve the information prior to possibly alerting anyone in the practice, and planned his actions prior to initiating anything out of the ordinary, he would likely have had his receipt books, patient files, and a working computer (or at least an electronic copy of the accounting system) to resolve his suspicions.

A written plan identifying the investigative approach and detailing each contemplated procedure is critical to ensure the completeness of an investigation.

Conducting the Procedures

Planning time is over, and it is time to go out and perform the procedures. Information, voluminous at times, will be collected, preserved, verified, analyzed, summarized, and maintained to support the findings. The keys to maintaining competency and integrity throughout the investigation are to remain organized and to document all pertinent activities and information. As documents are provided, develop a system to inventory and reference the documents so they will remain organized. This step is especially important when boxes upon boxes of records are provided. The same holds true for information provided electronically.

Document the information that was provided, where it was obtained or collected, who provided it, how it was provided, what happened to it once it was received, how it was inventoried and referenced, and where it was maintained after it was produced. Additionally, document how the information was verified, what procedures were performed with the information, what pertinent facts or results were identified, and any conclusions regarding the information. Ideally, the documentation should include what was received, what procedures were performed, the results of those procedures, and a conclusion.

Interviews are extremely useful procedures for gaining access to relevant information. Different forms of interviews can be used based on the goals of each interview. Interviews can range from being formal interrogations to casual discussions out in a warehouse. In a casual setting, the subject may not even be aware that he or she is being interviewed if the interview is done well. Documenting the particulars of each interview, as well as any information provided through the discussions, is critical to supporting the findings of the investigation.

Case Study 10.5 – Inventory on the Move

During a routine annual inventory observation for a regional distributor of lawn machinery, the auditors talked with the controller and chief financial officer (CFO) prior to interacting with the counting teams in the warehouses. The controller and CFO provided the auditors with a memo indicating no inventory was being received or shipped from any warehouse during the inventory-counting process. Therefore, nothing would be coming into the company or leaving until after the inventory count was completed and verified.

Before lunch, the auditors watched as count teams verified quantities on hand and completed inventory tags. Then the teams would write the items and amounts on their forms for each area. The auditors left for lunch while the count teams progressed through the warehouses.

On returning from lunch, the auditors went to the rear of the building, where they observed a flatbed trailer truck being loaded with new machinery. The auditors went over to the truck driver and started asking him questions about his truck, the items being loaded, and where the shipment was headed. The auditors also learned from the driver that a similar truck had left some time during the last hour. The auditors entered the warehouse through the loading area, only to find more machinery being prepared for shipping to customers. Through discussions with the shipping staff in the loading area, copies of invoices and bills of lading were provided to the auditors. Armed with this information, the auditors sought out the controller and CFO to discuss the memo provided earlier, regarding no shipping until the inventory was completed.

Needless to say that discussion didn't go so well, leading to the auditors' backing out of the audit engagement.

While procedures over financial records and electronic files are important in every investigation, never underestimate the importance of talking with individuals when conducting an investigation. Often it will be more productive to conduct interviews to gain information and only then turn to procedures on the documentation and files provided to corroborate, support, or refute the information provided in the interviews.

Findings

Every investigation results in some type of finding or conclusion. How these are communicated will vary for each investigation. In some cases, a formal report will be required; in others, a verbal report or informal memo summarizing the findings for the file will be all that is needed. Based on the strategy, objectives, and goals of the investigation, there may even be a reason for not writing a report.

Every report, regardless of form or purpose, should be written in such a way that it stands on its own. The report should also include at a minimum the following four sections:

1. Purpose of the investigation
2. Procedures performed
3. Results of those procedures
4. Conclusion

In writing a report, one must keep the audience in mind. Identifying the parties who will be reading and relying on the report, along with their level of financial knowledge, experience, and sophistication, will determine how technical the report is written. It is always better to minimize technical issues and accounting jargon and to write factually in plain English. When technical language cannot be avoided, do not assume the reader has sufficient knowledge of the subject to understand the references; include a paragraph explaining each term or issue. It may also be beneficial to use an analogy.

Consider the tense and person when writing, and keep these constant. A report that changes back and forth from past tense to present tense to past tense makes it harder for the reader to follow.

Depending on the purpose of your report, consider writing it in a matter-of-fact manner. For example, consider procedures performed to test compliance with a particular control or procedure. At the conclusion, the investigator or auditor would write a summary of the work performed along with any findings. It could be worded as follows:

I obtained and reviewed a copy of the internal control documentation regarding approving and recording general journal entries. I noted that the procedures over general journal entries required the completion and approval of a form, along with supporting information for each general journal entry. I next obtained a copy of the detailed general ledger report covering the month of December. I identified thirty (30) general journal entries posted to the general ledger in the month of December. I obtained access to the general journal entry forms and supporting details. I traced each of the thirty (30) general journal entries posted to a completed and approved form along with support. I identified five (5) general journal entries posted to the general ledger in December with no corresponding completed and approved form provided. I identified two (2) general journal entries posted to the general ledger in December for which the corresponding approved form did not contain the required supporting information. I concluded that compliance with the required procedures over approving and recording general journal entries was limited to twenty-three (23) out of thirty (30) posted entries.

Use of the Findings

Depending on the type and purpose of the investigation, what happens next will depend on the findings. In testing for compliance with controls and procedures, for example, any instances of noncompliance will likely lead to recommendations, which could include consequences for not complying with the expectations.

Remember the audience and the purpose when writing your report. Avoid technical terms, and when they can't be avoided, define them within your report. The less technical your report, the easier it will be for non-accountant readers to follow. Early in my career, I heard a speaker talk at a seminar about report writing. He stated that he wrote his reports from the perspective of a jury that might have no accounting background or experience, and on average a sixth-grade education. While that may not actually be the case, I have followed that guidance in writing my reports so that anyone can follow the actions I took, the findings I reached, and my conclusions.

Note

1. Garner, Bryan A. (ed.-in-chief), *Black's Law Dictionary* 8th edition (West, a Thomson Business: 2004).

CHAPTER 11

Fraud Investigation Alternatives

A s the previous authors of this book indicated, detecting fraud is difficult. Investigating fraud can be even more difficult, as well as costly. Individuals responsible for investigating fraud must be resourceful and innovative, creative and imaginative. But in reality, not every fraud will be investigated. In some cases of potential or even known fraud, the matter will be addressed without completing a full investigation. In other instances, the fraud will be allowed to continue, but will be monitored closely. Every case involves a number of issues to be considered, weighing the pros and cons of an investigation, determining the cost-benefit analysis, and identifying the potential consequences to all the stakeholders as a result of the full investigation.

Assessing the Feasibility of a Full Investigation

Whether fraud is only suspected or has actually occurred, inquiries should be made into the matter to collect facts that will be used to assess the feasibility of a full investigation. Identifying individuals or entities that may be involved in the matter is one of the first objectives. Determining what the scheme entails, how much money could be involved, how long it could have occurred, and whether there is any means of recovery are equally important objectives. However, much of this information may be easy to determine without a full investigation.

Minimizing the number of people involved in researching the potential matter will be critical to minimizing the risk that information could be leaked. If a potential target is tipped off or otherwise becomes aware that he or she may be the target of an investigation, there is a genuine risk that computer files could be deleted, hard drives and backup tapes destroyed, files and records shredded or discarded, and all other evidence destroyed. Maintaining confidentiality is critical to preserving the integrity of the potential investigation, as well as the integrity of individuals who may be involved.

Once basic preliminary information has been obtained to the fullest extent possible, a determination needs to be made as to whether or not the matter will be fully investigated. In making that determination, it is helpful to consider the goals and outcomes of the investigation, as well as to determine realistically what the victim organization is likely to do if in fact fraudulent activity is proven to have occurred and can be quantified. Will they seek criminal prosecution of the individuals as well as pursue civil remedies to collect the funds and costs due the organization, or will they simply terminate the individuals involved, implement better controls and procedures to prevent such a scenario from occurring in the future, and move forward?

Building upon the previous authors' considerations, the following five questions could be used as a guide in the determination process:

1. Do we initiate a full investigation to uncover every aspect of the potential scheme?
2. Do we initiate an investigation to uncover only the major aspects or specific elements of the potential scheme?
3. Do we hold on any investigation at this time but implement measures to monitor the potential scheme activity?
4. Do we skip an investigation entirely and focus efforts on evaluating the internal controls and procedures with the goal

of preventing the potential scheme from occurring in the future?

5. Do we do nothing and close out the potential matter?

If the fraud is too difficult to investigate or may require an inordinate amount of investigative effort, further investigation may not be a viable option. For example, if the amount of money involved in the potential fraud scheme is believed to be relatively small, expending resources in excess of the likely amount involved may not be a prudent decision. The difficulty lies in determining the potential amount that could be involved in the potential fraud scheme. Of course, in some situations the victim organization has no choice in the matter. The fraud must be fully investigated regardless of the amount of funds involved and the potential cost of conducting a complete investigation. This will likely be the case if the potential fraud scheme involves federal or state funds, trust accounts, client funds, and individuals holding political offices, to name a few examples.

The following case study best illustrates the merits of considering conducting a full investigation versus doing nothing.

Case Study 11.1 – How Deep Should You Dig to Uncover Fraud?

A client company discovered that its controller had been embezzling funds by writing manual checks to herself. The controller was terminated for insubordination and begged to keep her job. No wonder—within a few days of being fired, the month-end bank statement arrived in the mail. The owner of the company opened the bank statements and saw three manual checks made payable to the controller, which upon closer inspection had been concealed within bank loan accounts on the general ledger.

(Continued)

Historically, the bank statements had been received unopened directly by the controller, who removed any manual checks from the statements before forwarding them to the owner. Given the number of computer checks generated each month, along with batches of manual checks, it was no surprise that the owner had not noticed any missing checks. Once the statements were reviewed by the owner, they were returned to the same controller to perform the bank reconciliations. While such a lack of controls and segregation of duties may surprise you, it should be noted that this company's method of handling the bank statements and reconciliations is extremely common, especially within smaller organizations, closely held businesses, and family-run entities in which trust is implicit.

Under today's banking systems, few if any financial institutions still return the actual cancelled checks with the statements. Most banks converted years ago from actual cancelled checks to providing pages of the check images, often several to a page, front image only, and much too small to read. Many banks and vendors convert the checks received into electronic withdrawals from the payee's bank account and destroy the actual checks received. The electronic withdrawal is the only item that will appear on the payer's bank statements, and there will be no cancelled check or image provided by the bank, as they never saw the actual check. Still other institutions offer to provide a CD with check images, or allow customers to access their accounts online to view cancelled checks.

The client was faced with a feasibility determination. It was certain that the controller had taken around $7,000. Her employment had been terminated already for other reasons. How much had she taken? How long could she have been stealing? She had been there six years. Business had been brisk for awhile, but the company currently had a large bank overdraft, and its accountant said it was overspending on inventory.

The owner determined a fidelity bond of $500,000 was in place covering the controller. How much would it cost the company to fully investigate the theft? How far back should he go? What if he referred it to the authorities and the story hit the press? Would his customers think the company was in financial trouble? Also, just as crucial—what if the vendors thought they would not be able to pay their bills?

These are typical questions facing a business in this position, especially smaller businesses and nonprofit organizations.

After pondering the decision and meeting with counsel, the owner decided to press forward. The full investigation determined that the fraud scheme went back five years and extended to more than $600,000. With the assistance of law enforcement, the owner was able to discover checks that had been deposited directly into the controller's personal bank account. The evidence was overwhelming. There were copies of cancelled checks paid to the controller; the backs of the checks contained the controller's endorsement and personal bank account numbers; a lifestyle review uncovered a substantial house, cars, and lavish parties on a salary of about $45,000, with a husband on disability.

As a result of the full investigation of what had appeared initially to involve an amount less than $10,000, the fidelity bond carrier wrote the owner a check for $500,000. The controller was convicted in criminal court and received the better part of five years in jail. There was little publicity on the case, and the owner focused his efforts on bigger and better things within his business.

As you can see, for a short while the owner considered doing nothing, but in the end it was fortunate he decided to pursue the full investigation.

Clearly, this case is not typical of every potential fraud matter. Starting out with what appears to be a small case only to learn it is the tip of the iceberg is extremely common. However, having insurance coverage to enable the recovery of $500,000 on a theft of $600,000 is certainly not an everyday occurrence. In most cases, the funds are gone, and recovery is bleak at best.

In one of my embezzlement cases, we met with the target and her attorney to discuss the matter. The attorney indicated that his client had diverted close to $50,000 by stealing payments mailed to the company. After further investigative procedures were performed, we determined she embezzled just over $250,000, five times the amount she admitted to through her lawyer with her present during that meeting. Had we accepted their offer to resolve the matter based on her admission of $50,000, we would have never identified and recovered the additional $200,000 from the employee dishonesty insurance policy.

In my experience, I have had many victims tell me that while they were satisfied with the thoroughness of the investigation, they wished they had never known about all the items and issues identified through the investigation. They simply wished they could go back to a time before the scheme was detected, living their lives without ever knowing any of the details. This attitude is especially true when the fraud involves family members or long-term friendships. It is very difficult for victims to accept the fact that family or friends have committed fraud or stolen funds.

In some cases, not every aspect of the potential fraud scheme will be investigated. For reasons such as cost or availability of records, a better strategy will be to only investigate certain areas or aspects, or focus on the largest items.

Case Study 11.2 – Asleep at the Switch?

Just days before the annual meeting was to occur with the membership, the finance director for the congregation informed the treasurer on the board that the line of credit was maximized. This news came as a surprise to the treasurer, as he remembered the meeting held earlier in the year in which the finance director had reported to the board of directors that the line of credit had been repaid. Then he realized he had been asking for updated financial reports in preparation for the annual meeting for quite some time, and he had grown frustrated with the finance director's delays. Now the treasurer was faced with a question he couldn't answer—how could the congregation's line of credit with the bank be maximized if it had been repaid and no recent advances had been approved by the board?

The treasurer started reviewing the bank records and other financial documents, only to learn that the congregation's bank account balances were significantly lower than the amounts reported recently by the finance director. After the treasurer made a call to the congregation's attorney, the finance director was placed on paid administrative leave and escorted from the building.

Recent loan statements were found in an unorganized stack of papers on a shelf behind the finance director's desk. The loan documents themselves were found in manila folders on his desk, along with various bank statements, deposit receipts, and credit card statements. A quick scan of the loan information revealed two significant items. First, the congregation's line of credit had been increased in the spring by $100,000. Second, advances had been made against the line since the increase throughout the summer and fall, bringing

(Continued)

the outstanding balance to the maximum limit. The treasurer wondered who had approved the line increase as well as the advances, and became nervous about what had happened to the proceeds from each advance.

The credit card statements included cards in the name of the congregation as well as other cards in the name of the finance director. Many of the statements were missing, but based on the ones located in his office, there appeared to be personal charges included on both types of cards.

The deposit receipts identified various deposits made to bank accounts unknown to the treasurer. A report was generated from the congregation's general ledger identifying all the deposits made during the last six months. The treasurer attempted to match the deposit receipts to deposits listed on the report, and found many of the deposits found on the desk did not match deposits on the report. The finance director's status was quickly converted from paid to unpaid administrative leave.

The treasurer convinced the other board members that a complete fraud investigation was required. One of the first procedures performed was an inventory of the finance director's workspace areas. All financial records were collected and grouped, and any missing documents were sought from outside sources, such as requesting missing bank statements from the banks. A request was made for the missing credit card statements, but none were ever provided by the financial institutions, as they would only provide them to the individual named on the account—who happened to be the finance director for every charge account. The bank statements received only went back seven years, and in many instances the bank was unable to provide complete copies as well as many deposit details or images of identified checks.

All of the loans and the line of credit were traced back to inception. The treasurer learned that the board had approved adding the finance director as an authorized signer to the line of credit two years earlier, which is how he had been able to increase the credit limit. Each loan was reconciled and agreed with the activity reported on the general ledger. All advances and repayments were identified for the line of credit and traced to entries on the general ledger, as well as to deposits and checks within other bank accounts.

Through a review of all the financial records located or provided, it was determined that the Finance Director likely had diverted deposits from the congregation to personal accounts, charged personal items on credit cards paid by the congregation, and used advances from the line of credit to cover the thefts. However, after months and months of seeking the required documentation from the financial institutions, little useful information was ever produced.

Disappointed and frustrated that sufficient information could not be procured to pursue the finance director beyond his obvious breach of fiduciary duties to the congregation, the board made the tough decision to cut their losses, end the investigation, and simply terminate the finance director's employment.

Monitoring Operational Areas at Risk of Fraud

In some instances, sufficient information is not known to allow for the determination if a potential fraud scheme is occurring. A great example of this is when an anonymous tip is received indicating a fraud is occurring. The tip may or may not include details, and often the tip simply implicates an individual doing something illegal or inconsistent with company policies and procedures. However, it is not uncommon for individuals to leave tips that are without basis simply to jam up another individual—perhaps a co-worker or supervisor.

Based on the information received, an investigation may or may not be initiated. Often, other procedures are implemented to monitor a situation to determine if there is any merit to the tip received. Surveillance may be conducted, video monitoring could be used, and other measures can be implemented to determine if in fact the reported fraudulent activity is occurring. In much the same way as law enforcement treats a report of potential criminal activity, the agency may conduct surveillance, have individuals wear wires to capture conversations, or obtain wire taps to monitor phone conversations if it wants to catch an individual in the act or corroborate the information received.

Based on what is learned from monitoring the activity, a determination will need to be made at some point to either conduct a fraud investigation or simply close out the matter and move on.

Case Study 11.3 – Walking Parts

A local manufacturer implemented cycle counts to improve the accuracy of its inventory counts. Prior to the commencement of cycle counts, the computerized inventory system commonly showed there was a particular part in stock. The staff would go to the shelf location to pull the part, only to find there were none on hand. When the cycle counts did not improve the situation, the company installed fencing surrounding the parts location, along with a locked gate. This measure was designed to prevent just anyone from pulling parts from inventory. Now, anyone who wanted to pull parts needed to unlock the cage each time to gain access to the actual parts on the shelves. Only the staff authorized to pull parts were provided access to the gate.

One month after the cage was installed, a physical inventory was taken. The results of the inventory showed that parts listed in the computer were still not on hand. Despite the drastic measures taken, along with the costs incurred to secure the inventory, little had changed.

Convinced there could be no other explanation than that someone with access to the parts inventory cage was stealing the parts, management decided to conduct covert surveillance over the parts inventory area. Secretly, during the middle of the night, a discrete camera system was installed, with monitoring made available only to the chief financial officer and the business owner.

On the very first day of monitoring, a parts supervisor was seen entering the secured caged area, selecting parts from the shelves and taking them back to his office. The supervisor was never seen coming out of his office with the parts, so the owner went to his office to determine what had happened to the parts. The owner found that the supervisor had placed the parts in a gym bag on the floor behind his desk. Without the use of surveillance to monitor the parts cage, it is highly unlikely the owner would have ever identified the supervisor who was stealing the inventory. The supervisor admitted to taking the items in his bag, but stated that it was the first time he had done anything like that. He never admitted to taking any other items and was terminated that day. No procedures could be performed to quantify all the prior thefts he likely committed, and a criminal complaint was initiated based solely on the items found in his bag that day.

Revamping Internal Controls: Closing the Barn Door

Aside from internal controls that are designed primarily to ensure the integrity of an entity's accounting system, some internal controls are designed to be fraud specific. The objective of fraud-specific internal controls is to prevent or deter future fraud from occurring.

Depending on the nature of a potential fraud scheme, as well as the feasibility of performing a complete fraud investigation, it is not unusual for a potential victim organization to decide not to perform the investigation but rather to focus efforts on evaluating the internal controls and procedures, with the goal of implementing better controls to prevent future fraud schemes. Factors that could lead a victim organization to this decision include the potential cost considerations of the investigation, the realistic likelihood of collecting any restitution if in fact a fraud had been committed, and the potential ramifications to the organization should information about the potential fraud scheme or investigation make its way into the public. The nature of the organization also needs to be considered. For any publicly traded company, merely the news that a fraud inquiry has been initiated, for any reason, could have a potentially devastating and irreversible impact on the organization's stock prices, even if the potential fraud matter proves to be unfounded. Look at the case of public accounting giant Arthur Andersen around the time of the Enron issue. Andersen was charged with obstruction of justice for potentially shredding documents related to Enron, which in part led to the closing of their doors. Well after their demise, the charges against Andersen were dropped. However, the damage was done—and it was irreversible. That's not to say Andersen was right or wrong in their actions, but certainly Andersen should not have suffered such a significant loss, especially if they never were shown to have done anything wrong.

Each potential fraud matter must be assessed based on the facts and issues present. As part of the feasibility assessment, the potential consequences to the victim organization have to be identified and weighed against the benefit of conducting the investigation. If, for example, the victim organization is a nonprofit charity financially dependent on people sending them donations, the potential negative impact that news of an employee embezzlement could have on their future fundraising efforts might easily outweigh the benefit of pursuing a potential fraud matter. The same holds true for religious organizations. News of a potential fraud committed by a spiritual leader could prove devastating, both financially and politically. Members would be less likely to continue contributing at the same levels, if at all, if they learned their funds were being diverted.

Whatever the compelling reasons not to pursue a complete fraud investigation, efforts are often focused on identifying the controls and procedures that failed to prevent the potential fraud scheme as well as identifying measures that can be practically implemented to prevent the fraud scheme from ever happening again.

Case Study 11.4 – No More Press!

The assistant controller for a local school was responsible for many financial areas, including tuition management. The school's tuition system was internalized to save money by not using an outside vendor, and the assistant controller's duties included invoicing families, collecting payments, determining financial aid assistance, and managing the unpaid balances.

Tuition payments could be mailed or brought to the school. Any payment received outside the mail was

(Continued)

memorialized within the prenumbered, three-part receipt book. One receipt was provided to the family, one copy was attached to the payment and maintained with the other payments for the day, and the third copy remained within the receipt book. The payments were then left in the mail slot for the assistant controller to retrieve, endorse, process for deposit, and post to the family's balance on the system.

During a planned absence, a family came to the school to pay their tuition. They brought with them their latest statement received from the school, along with receipts they were provided in the past for earlier tuition payments. They stated that their statement was incorrect, as it did not reflect all the payments they had made for the school year.

Upon review of their statement and information, the controller agreed with the family. The family was given a receipt for their payment and thanked for identifying the problem with their statement.

The controller traced the family's receipts to the receipt book and matched the copies to the ones in the books. He then reviewed the postings on the family's account within the system and noted that the tuition payments made in cash had never been reflected on the family's account.

Troubled by this finding, the controller looked at other families who paid their tuitions in cash. Other families' accounts had similar discrepancies to the first family. The controller attempted to trace the cash payments into actual bank deposits but was unable to trace all the cash receipts to the bank deposits.

By comparing the receipts in the receipt books to the postings in family accounts on the system, it was determined that someone was collecting payments but not reflecting the payments in the family accounts.

A complete fraud investigation was initiated, and close to $100,000 was identified as being collected and receipted, but never reflected on the family's tuition accounts. It was determined that the assistant controller had signed the receipts for many of the cash payments received from families. Further, it was determined that the same cash payments were never included in any of the organization's deposits. Lastly, it was proven that no one else within the organization had similar access and opportunity, and that it was highly likely the assistant controller was stealing the cash payments from the school.

In discussing these findings with counsel and the stakeholders, it was learned that the school had received a significant amount of negative publicity less than a year ago. Although not financially related, just the fact that they were in the media and received such negative publicity was sufficient for them to want to avoid any publicity at all.

Doing Nothing?

Are there circumstances where it would be prudent to do nothing to suppress or disclose a fraud scheme that it is believed will continue? The answer is yes. Many people may find it disturbing that a fraud has occurred or may even be occurring and they have no ability or desire to stop it. While it may not be an acceptable practice within a government agency or involving government employees and politicians, it happens all too often in the private sector.

As wrong as it might sound, the fraud investigator is an objective fact finder who typically works for the victim organization or company. What happens with the information produced through investigative measures is not usually the fraud investigator's call. In the end, even if the victim solicits input from the fraud professional, the victim typically has sole discretion to decide what, if anything, they want to do with the information.

However bizarre it may seem, doing nothing is sometimes the most prudent decision. Nevertheless, the fraudulent activity should never be simply forgotten. It should be monitored regularly to ensure that it remains within the victim's tolerable limits.

Many banks, restaurants, and retail stores may find themselves in these situations, especially considering the difficulty of obtaining qualified replacement candidates for employees who otherwise perform well. Reviewing and reconciling the daily activity of employees could reveal they are stealing petty amounts. However, considering that the individual may be paid at a low hourly rate, is responsible, is never late for his or her shifts, performs his or her job responsibilities adequately or better, and is great with the customers, chances are the owner will not want to call this individual on the carpet. The risk of losing an otherwise good employee, and the unknown factor of how a replacement hire will perform, will almost always outweigh the cost of doing business by retaining the individual. Often, the victim has no practical alternative other than doing nothing but monitor the shortages to ensure that they do not exceed tolerable limits.

Case Study 11.5 – Cost of Sales

A distributor with annual sales close to $100 million depended on a lean sales staff to generate orders and maintain customer relations. One sales manager in particular had been with the company for nearly ten years and was their top producer. In the last fiscal year, the sales manager and his sales team of two individuals were responsible for generating more than 70% of the company's sales orders. The sales manager was well compensated by the company and was held in very high regard by the owners. He was provided with a company credit card but was required to comply with company policies prohibiting the use of the company card for personal expenses.

Month after month, the accounting department reviewed the monthly credit card statements, and each month, each cardholder's portion was distributed to each individual cardholder for approval as well as submission of the supporting receipts.

Every cardholder returned their approved statement along with supporting receipts except for the sales manager. Month after month, the accounting department grew frustrated by the sales manager's lack of compliance with company policies. It became apparent that the sales manager was using his card for personal purchases.

Eventually, the accounting department brought this issue to the attention of the owner. The owner reviewed the information compiled, including copies of the sales manager's monthly statements, and listened to his accounting staff complain that the sales manager never complied and ignored request after request for the approved statements and supporting receipts.

The owner determined the magnitude of personal expenses charged and paid by the company was negligible in comparison to what the sales manager and his team brought to the company in the form of sales volume (over $70 million in the last year alone) and customer support, and decided that he would not require the sales manager to comply with the credit card policies. Rather, the owner instructed the accounting staff to continue monitoring the

(Continued)

> sales manager's charge activity, discontinue pursuing him for the return of his statement and supporting receipts, and inform the owner if the sales manager's activity or amounts significantly increased beyond the existing levels.

In the first section of this book, fraud was defined, various aspects of fraud were discussed, and many common financial fraud schemes were identified. The next section identified external and internal responses to the growing fraud issue, addressing the need for new measures to be implemented to reverse the trends relative to the size and frequency of fraud schemes. The last section discussed investigative issues and alternatives in response to fraud schemes that are detected.

In the battle on fraud, it is paramount that every fraud scheme be detected and stopped as early as possible to minimize a victim's loss. Once detected, the victim and the investigator must review the known facts and circumstances of the scheme and collectively decide if the matter is worth investigating and prosecuting. The investigation decision will be made on a case-by-case basis, depending on factors such as available evidence and resources, as well as the potential cost versus the benefit associated with a complete investigation. In some cases, a fraud scheme may not be investigated or prosecuted at all.

The Appendices that follow include three case studies based on actual fraud schemes. Each case details how the fraud scheme was perpetrated as well as how it was detected and investigated. The cases were included to illustrate complete fraud investigations using real-world examples.

In closing, remember that fraud affects everyone. Although you may not have been personally victimized through a direct loss of funds by each scheme perpetrated, the costs of fraud schemes are always passed along to consumers in the form of higher insurance premiums, higher medical costs, higher taxes, and higher costs of goods and services consumed. We all must remember that we have a personal role in preventing and/or detecting fraudulent activity. Remain vigilant, or risk becoming a victim to fraud due to complacency. In the words of the late Ronald Reagan, "Trust, but verify."[1]

Note

1. "Trust But Verify." *Opinion. The New York Times.* Published Thursday December 10, 1987. Here's a link: www.nytimes.com/ 1987/ 12/10/opinion/trust-but-verify.html

Vending

It was scheduled as a routine audit of the inventory and customer accounts receivable balances. The financial institution had extended credit to the business in the form of collateral-based lending, whereby the amount of outstanding debt was dependent on the level and strength of the collateral. In this case, the collateral was the company's inventory and receivables. The company was required to submit monthly inventory details and customer account receivable aging reports to the bank, and both were used to calculate the maximum amount of borrowing available. The company also provided annual audited financial statements issued by a regional public accounting firm within three months of its December year-end.

Although the audit had been scheduled and confirmed in advance, upon the auditor's arrival the owner of the business was nowhere to be found. An hour later, the owner arrived and met with the auditors. Brief introductions were made to various personnel, and the owner left the auditors in a crowded office with stacks of printed reports to review. Within a short period, the auditors determined the reports were old and irrelevant for the planned procedures and sought out the owner. Once again, the owner could not be located.

The auditors, not wanting to waste time by waiting, turned to the staff and started asking for information. One of the auditors sat at an empty desk in the business office reviewing the current accounts receivable aging report provided by one of the staff. While working at the desk, the auditor observed one of the billing clerks at the desk immediately in front open her top drawer of her desk. In the drawer was a large stack of currency that later turned out to be nearly $50,000. The auditor asked the clerk if large amounts of currency were maintained in the building. The clerk stated she kept enough to make change in her desk, and the remaining cash was stored in a safe in the back. The clerk brought the auditor to the back and showed him the location of the safe.

Later in the morning, the business office door opened and in walked a man dressed in a long coat carrying a grocery bag. The man sat in a chair situated next to the woman's desk, and the man proceeded to retrieve currency from the bag. He provided the stacks of currency to the clerk, signed a slip, and left with his empty grocery bag. Throughout the day, two similar men visited and provided cash to the clerk.

While reviewing the aging report, the auditor noticed that many of the customer balances were more than 60 days old. This was an important finding, as the bank's lending formula only allowed borrowing on accounts less than 60 days old. Comparing the aging report to several monthly reports provided historically by the customer showed that no accounts over 60 days previously existed. The auditor, still waiting on the return of the owner, asked for and received a copy of the detailed general ledger report for the most recent period. On the general ledger were significant sales returns, along with general journal entries posted to accounts receivable.

The owner finally resurfaced just before lunch. The owner's wife arrived at the company and interrupted the meeting with the auditors. As the owner placed a lunch order for himself and his wife, he removed a large roll of currency from his pants pocket. He peeled off a few $20 bills and gave them to his wife for the lunch order, and then put the roll back into his pocket.

Having seen enough for the morning, the auditors decided to take a break and leave for lunch, mainly to discuss their observations.

Leaving by the side door, the auditors walked past the owner's wife's Mercedes Benz, a special two-seat model later estimated to cost $120,000. The auditors scanned the parking lot for the owner's car and noticed a second high-end luxury car parked hidden behind the dumpster. The auditors noted that the car had not been there in the morning and must have been the owner's.

In the afternoon, the auditors went out to the warehouse to review the inventory on hand and talk with inventory personnel. They asked one of the individuals in the warehouse how often products were returned from customers. The individual responded that customers almost never returned products, and if they did, the returns consisted of small quantities of items mainly for spoilage. The auditors asked him when the last time a large return was processed, and the individual stated that it had been maybe a year or two ago, with the closing of several stores by one of their customers. He said there hadn't been a large return in quite some time. The information he provided was in direct contradiction with the entries recorded in the current month alone on the company's general ledger. The auditors then asked for copies of any return documentation or credit memos, and the individual provided copies of the last ten return forms. The forms were consistent with what he had told them.

Armed with this information, the auditors sought out the owner to discuss their unexpected findings. The owner, still casual and cavalier in his attitude, led the auditors to the small crowded office. The auditors asked him about product returns, and asked him to provide copies of all the documentation supporting all product returns and credit memos issued in the last 60 days. Suddenly, the owner was much more nervous; he quickly closed the door and explained that he couldn't find the paperwork. He stated that he, too, was looking for the paperwork in anticipation of the audit, and that he was unable to locate any of it. He also stated that his system couldn't reproduce the forms and documentation.

The auditors asked the owner how he kept track of the returns and other adjustments posted to accounts receivable, and he removed a spiral bound pad from his desk. He stated that he kept track of all his sales, sales returns, and customer payments in his notebook. The auditors' quick glance through the notebook for recent entries clearly showed that the activity posted within the company's accounting system was much different from that shown in his notebook.

The auditors asked the owner for a copy of his notebook, but he refused to provide any copies. He stated that the same information existed within his general ledger system, which had already been provided.

The auditors then asked him about the currency transactions. The owner stated that many of his customers preferred to pay their accounts receivable balance in cash, rather than by check. He stated the customer was given a written receipt for every payment, and the payments were tracked within his notebook.

The auditors stopped their procedures and thanked the owner for his time. Then they regrouped to review their findings and the owner's representations and determine a new course of action. They determined that, at a minimum, the owner was committing tax fraud for not reporting cash transactions over $10,000. He was also likely underreporting sales and income to minimize taxes owed at every level.

The nature of the findings raised suspicions about the completeness, accuracy, and integrity of the financial information the owner provided about the company each month to the bank, as well as the completeness, accuracy, and integrity of their annual audited financial statements. The auditors asked one of the clerks about her past experiences with auditors. The clerk stated that the auditing firm would send out a very inexperienced staff accountant to do the audit. The auditor sat in the crowded office with a stack of documents provided by the owner and never interacted with any of the other personnel during the entire time spent at the company. The clerk stated that no one from the firm with any significant experience had ever come to the company, and no one had asked them any questions. She stated the first time anyone sat outside the office and interacted with anyone from the company was that very day, when the auditors arrived to do the audit for the bank.

The auditors summarized their findings and forwarded their report to the bank. In response to the findings, the bank met with the owner, reviewed the issues, and agreed that the company would need to find another bank to assume the obligations. Within a few months, a new bank sent out auditors to perform due diligence procedures, and within a month of their visit, the loan was fully paid to the bank from the proceeds of a refinance with the other financial institution.

Although they were happy for their client bank, which had successfully removed itself from a potentially bad situation and collected the full amount of its loans, the auditors were amazed that the loan had been refinanced, especially after external auditors were brought in to perform due diligence procedures.

Lessons Learned

The following recommendations will aid auditors in discovering issues outside a client's records and reports:

- *Rely on your observation skills.* Paying attention to the surroundings and environment will often provide many clues to what really happens. In the case above, the auditors observed the expensive cars, customer transactions in cash, large amounts of cash in the owner's pocket, and the currency in the staff member's drawer. Had the auditors simply remained in the small office and worked through the reports and other information, it is likely they never would have noticed any of those clues. This may explain how the subsequent due diligence allowed the owner to refinance the loans.

- *Don't let clients or targets dictate how and where you work.* Clients often like to dictate how and where you will perform your procedures. It is a fine line between trusting a client and allowing them to control the entire audit process and procedures. In situations in which fraud is occurring, it is common for the target to limit the auditor's access to information that could lead to detection. In a respectful way, auditors need to find ways to work outside the client's box to learn things that might otherwise never be identified. In my most recent inventory observation performed in public accounting, the owners requested that we come and go through the company's main front door entrance. The same owners stated that no inventory was moving in or out of the company during the inventory. Upon returning from lunch, we decided to enter through the rear of the building. As we rounded the corner of the parking lot, we observed a trailer truck loaded with inventory preparing to leave. The driver stated that a similar truck had left an hour earlier. In the shipping area were workers preparing to ship more items. Needless to say, the owners were less than happy that we had entered through the back of the building.

- *Talk with the workers.* In most if not all cases, the rank-and-file workers are not aware of fraud occurring, especially if it is financial statement fraud being committed by the owners or senior management. If you seek them out and ask them questions about their jobs and activity in their areas, they will generally answer you honestly, as they are unaware of what you are asking and why you are asking it, and they have not been told in advance to not answer any questions. I recommend that you go out into the warehouses and talk to employees in the field and on the lines, from receiving through shipping. You will learn much about how things have really been run at the company.

- *Corroborate what you learn.* Compare the information you collect through observations and discussions with employees to the activity reflected and reported in the company's financial reports and statements. Often, if fraud is being perpetrated, depending on what fraud scheme is involved, the information will not be consistent, leading to additional procedures.

Living a Façade

J oanne Spencer had worked at Smart Living Furniture for eight years. She had started when it was struggling to survive and had lived through the lean years before the company began to prosper. Trusted and respected, Spencer was the corporate accountant, bookkeeper, and office manager rolled into one. She made $57,000 a year, supervised several people, and reported directly to the owner, Tom Bradford. Her duties included paying vendors, depositing receipts, and reconciling bank accounts for the company, which had more than 180 employees. The company had one owner, Bradford, who made all the key decisions in the company, and a regional CPA firm provided basic financial statement compilation and tax services.

Spencer was a divorced single mother of two girls in their mid-20s, one still in college. Her house was modest but impeccably decorated; she had added a pool in the year before the fraud discovery. She always drove a newer model expensive car, and her clothes were trendy and fashionable. When a group of employees went out for a meal or drinks, Spencer always picked up the tab.

Spencer's downfall began during yet another expensive European vacation. When she went on vacation, she was very careful to prepay bills, take care of petty cash requirements, and in short, eliminate the need for anyone to be in her office when she was gone. While Spencer was absent, a fill-in employee, who needed petty cash, noticed something unusual while reimbursing the petty cash account. She realized that Spencer was writing large reimbursement checks from the company to the petty cash account each week that far exceeded supporting expense receipts. She notified Bradford, who in turn informed his accountant who began an inquiry that turned into an investigation.

When Spencer returned from vacation, the company's owner confronted her with the petty cash discrepancies. At first Spencer denied any wrongdoing, but when the owner offered not to press charges in return for a full confession and documentation of how much she had stolen, Spencer quickly relented. She admitted taking approximately $5,000 over a one-year period; however, this was only the tip of the iceberg.

Emotions were running high in the company over their disbelief that Joanne Spencer, a dear friend and colleague, could ever steal from the company. People in the company at all levels were experiencing, to one degree or another, the four mental states triggered by fraud detection: denial, then anger, resentment, and finally acceptance. At first they could not believe Spencer would steal and they felt her betrayal personally. As anger set in, there was a strong sense that she should be punished, the more quickly the better. Often, when these feelings boil up, premature and damaging actions can result, such as the leveling of accusations that cannot be proven.

Smart Living was insured for employee dishonesty. To help quantify the loss and prepare a proof of loss for the insurer, the company retained forensic accountants. By engaging outside expertise, Bradford benefited from an objective approach, which ensured that proper fraud investigation steps were taken. Even more important, Bradford learned the complete truth of Spencer's activities, which far exceeded those to which she had admitted. Spencer refused to assist the financial investigators; that raised their suspicions. Through interviews with Smart

Living's staff, the investigators learned of Spencer's lavish lifestyle, which included tales of opulent parties, state-of-the-art audio and video equipment, renovations to her house, expensive vacations, and a penchant for expensive new cars. Clearly Spencer was living beyond her apparent financial means. This information led the investigators to look into her financial transactions at work involving more than just petty cash.

The investigation revealed that Spencer indeed was stealing money through petty cash. She reused expense receipts, created fictitious receipts, altered receipts, and did not provide an accounting or reconciliation of the system. The investigation also discovered that Spencer was writing company checks for her own personal benefit. Spencer was an authorized signer on the corporate operating checking accounts. The forensic accountants performed an inventory of her office and discovered that she had the facsimile signatory stamp of the owner in her possession to add his signature on checks as required for check amounts over $500. Spencer included her own American Express bill with payments for Smart Living's corporate accountant, and paid many of her personal expenses with company checks.

Each check Spencer signed was painstakingly examined from the operating account to determine if it was used for business or personal purposes. A credit check performed by the forensic accountants revealed that Spencer was heavily in debt, and many of her listed credit card companies were found to be payees on the company's operating account.

When the investigation was completed, it was apparent that Spencer had been paying personal expenses with company funds and had diverted cash from the company's petty cash account. These findings were corroborated with replacement statements obtained from the credit card companies and other vendors in order to file a proof-of-loss with the insurance company and for possible use in support of a criminal prosecution.

According to the forensic accountant's investigation, Spencer embezzled approximately $500,000 from the company over a seven-year period. Spencer originally admitted to stealing only $5,000, or one percent, of this amount when she was first caught and confronted.

Although other areas were examined for fraud, such as payroll, vendor invoice files, computer records, and purchasing, it was determined that the bulk of Spencer's theft occurred from the company's petty cash and operating account. Spencer was able to perpetrate her schemes in both areas because there were no internal controls implemented at Smart Living and no one independently reviewed her work.

Spencer may have committed other frauds within the company, but the investigation was discontinued because the insurance coverage limitations had been exceeded. Bradford decided against incurring additional costs just to document more fraud, although the company considered recovery of the excess loss against Spencer personally. An asset search performed by the forensic accountants determined she had insufficient assets for a civil recovery suit. An insurance claim was filed along with the forensic accountant's report, which was also provided to the police to support criminal charges against Spencer. The investigation and resulting report produced a winning situation for both Smart Living and the police, although the loss of Spencer as a trusted employee rocked company morale. Bradford recovered several hundred thousand dollars from the insurance policy and was able to deduct the loss on its tax return. Spencer was prosecuted, entered a guilty plea, and was sentenced to 18 months in jail. The success of this case was highly attributable to the work of the forensic accountants. The police, who typically do not possess the training, experience, and capacity to investigate such a case, were provided a professionally prepared forensic report needed to support their case.

Prevention Techniques

The following recommendations could have limited Smart Living's exposure to fraud schemes such as the one perpetrated by Spencer:

- *Communicate management's philosophy.* Communication between owners, management, and employees regarding fraud should be clear and concise. The consequences of committing fraud should be communicated and understood by all employees of the company. If employees have personal problems or financial concerns, management should be available to listen and assist the individual to the extent practical. Open communications may reduce the risk of certain frauds, particularly the schemes in which employees steal because of personal financial pressures. Fraud schemes motivated by greed may be deterred by management's strong commitment to terminate and prosecute any wrongdoing by employees.
- *Document policies and procedures.* Written codes, policies, and procedures prescribe how employees should behave and perform their assigned responsibilities. Is it okay to accept gifts from clients? Can old company equipment be taken home? Can expenses be paid without receipts? When should customers' accounts be written off? Providing detailed and documented policies and procedures to all employees throughout the company not only sets the tone and expectations for employees to follow, but also eliminates an employee's response of, "I didn't know," if something goes wrong.
- *Implement internal controls.* Segregation of duties among people and departments is a primary internal control. Many smaller companies, however, cannot afford to hire additional people or have difficulty in splitting responsibilities.

In these instances, owners can be used to implement compensating controls. Sales and shipping, receipts of cash and bank deposits, and check writing and bank reconciliations are all important duties that require segregation and oversight. Spencer was able to perpetrate her crimes for so long because there were no internal controls over her areas of responsibility. She wrote the checks, recorded the checks in the ledger, received the bank statements, and reconciled the checkbook. She even had the facsimile stamp of the owner in her office. Because the company was growing and had many vendors, nobody noticed the additional $100,000 in "additional" payments Spencer made to herself each year through her various schemes.

- *Conduct employee screening.* "An ounce of prevention is worth a pound of cure." A basic background check is inexpensive, can highlight potential risks to the company, and can act as an integrity check to representations in the prospect employees' resume. In today's hiring environment inaccuracies and omissions are common on resumes and job applications. Employers should independently verify all references, past employers, educational degrees, and licenses held. During the investigation, Spencer's resume was reviewed, and her last former employer was contacted. Her past employer informed the forensic accountants that Spencer was "asked to leave" after certain questionable financial transactions were discovered. The company never further investigated these transactions, choosing to deal with the issue by not dealing with it. As a result, Spencer obtained the same type of job with Smart Living as she had held for her prior employer. A simple background check could have exposed this issue prior to hiring Spencer.
- *Verify all work performed.* Implement a process whereby individuals internal or external to the company review transactions and activity, monitor employee behavior, and verify

records on a regular or periodic basis. These controls act as powerful deterrents to fraud. Even if the outside accounting firm provides only minimal services to the company, they may be able to help with designing, implementing, and monitoring internal controls to minimize the risk of fraud.

- *Review adequacy of insurance coverage.* Obtain employee dishonesty, employee crime, or fidelity insurance coverage in an amount sufficient to allow the company to recover from a significant theft or embezzlement. This coverage is relatively inexpensive for large amounts of coverage and can be controlled through the deductible.

Appendix C

Disappearing Inventory

James Jensen, CPA, known as JJ to his friends, was a member of the fraud investigation team for Alpha Distributions, Inc. Having completed three years with the fraud team, JJ was experienced in investigative techniques and often relied on symptoms identified in ordinary business operations that indicated potential fraudulent activity.

Among other activities, Alpha distributed a high-quality line of hand and power tools. The last three physical inventory counts of the tool inventory had revealed disturbing significant shortages. Alpha's average inventory for hand and power tools during the three-year period approximated $50 million. The inventory counts obtained during the last three physical inventories revealed shortages of 4%, 6%, and 8%, respectively. After the 4% shortage was discovered, Alpha management was understandably concerned, but willing to accept the various rationalizations offered. When the shortage increased to 6% a year later, Alpha's management became convinced that it was experiencing a serious theft problem, but was unable to determine how the tools were leaving the warehouses. All security measures were reviewed, and merchandise staged for shipment was double-checked and periodically spot-checked before being loaded onto the trailers.

In an attempt to determine explanations for the inventory count discrepancies, Alpha installed video cameras at the entrance and exit points. Controls over merchandise shipping were strengthened, and warehouse security was added. When the third physical inventory count revealed an increase from 6% to 8% in the disparity between the physical counts and the book inventory, Alpha's management was understandably upset.

JJ was assigned to determine the cause of the inventory discrepancies. He began his inquiry by reviewing the policies and procedures used to conduct each of the three physical inventory counts but found nothing unusual or unreasonable. He reviewed the security measures implemented by Alpha subsequent to the initial disclosures of the inventory shortages and found them to be appropriate and adequate. In fact, he found some measures to be excessive, in that the checking and rechecking of outgoing shipments often delayed the shipments, resulting in the drivers complaining about the long waits. The measures were also found to be very labor intensive and costly.

JJ reviewed video of the shipping areas for selected days and found that the dock areas were crowded with competing incoming and outgoing shipments. However, after a careful review of all control measures and hours of videotapes, JJ could see no reason for taking exception to the procedures followed. All shipments appeared to be diligently checked and double-checked as required. He reviewed the entire inventory control system, starting with the processing of incoming orders by the sales department. JJ continued through the preparation of sales and shipping documents, distribution of the documents to the warehouse authorizing the removal of stock from warehouse inventories, and the accounting department's inventory control processes, which were used for recording changes in inventory balances and posting sales to accounts receivable. JJ's evaluation failed to identify any opportunities for inventory shortages.

Focusing on the crowded shipping docks, JJ went back to the videotapes and watched them for many more hours, hoping to find a lapse in the controls. While watching the tapes of the shipping dock areas, JJ inadvertently inserted a tape of the receiving dock areas. JJ observed personnel from the receiving dock area being drawn to the shipping dock to complete the extra controls being exercised over merchandise being shipped out to customers from that dock. The result, however, was clearly evident in the videotapes. Workers in the receiving area were not thoroughly checking incoming receipts. JJ observed several pallets of tools that were unloaded from trailers that only received a cursory review rather than a conscientious opening and counting of the actual quantities that were received.

JJ speculated on the possibility that if inbound shipments contained less than the quantities indicated on the bills of lading and receiving documents, and if receiving dock personnel did not catch these shortages, then this lapse in compliance to receiving procedures could account for the disparity between book inventories and physical counts. In basic terms, if 1,000 impact drivers were listed on the packing slips and receiving documents and were marked as received, when only 900 drivers were actually received but went unnoticed by Alpha's personnel, then a shortage would surface during a physical inventory. Alpha's inventory records would reflect 1,000 as received when in fact only 900 were received. JJ was skeptical that this could be the explanation for the inventory discrepancies, as it would mean Alpha's suppliers constantly undershipped quantities to account for the overall 8% inventory shrinkage.

JJ began by preparing a flow chart that depicted the procedure for controlling and recording incoming shipments into the warehouses. JJ quickly determined how a theft of goods received could go undetected. To test his theory, JJ selected a number of recent receiving reports retrieved from the warehouse files, noted the storage locations indicated on the receiving reports, and went into the warehouse to verify the quantities. Verification was not a problem. The actual receiving pallets were still intact, as the warehouse picked items to be shipped on a first in, first out basis, meaning the oldest inventory was picked before more recently received items. He was able to trace the specific incoming shipments and found no exceptions in the counts. However, he discovered that 5% of the receiving reports reviewed contained notations that a partial shipment had been received. Individuals reviewing shipments received discovered that the shipper had delivered fewer items than were expected to be received. JJ carefully examined all the receiving reports he had selected in which Alpha had received less than the complete order. In every case, he found the shipping source was either highly reputable or the receipts were coming from Alpha's own manufacturing facilities. What interested JJ most, however, was that all of the partial shipments were delivered by the same freight carrier.

When he questioned the warehouse manager about the partial orders, he explained to JJ that the practice of receiving partial shipments was not all that unusual. He stated sometimes it occurred because two or more trucks were required, or at times when Alpha indicated an urgent need for an item, the shipper sent out any available inventory for the item ordered, with plans to ship the balance of items at a later date. When less than the complete order was received, the receiving dock marked the quantity that was actually delivered.

JJ was curious to know whether the partial shipments could somehow explain the inventory shortages disclosed. He tested his theory by inserting into his flowchart of receiving procedures a hypothetical instance in which 1,000 items were ordered but only 900 were received. JJ was convinced that any shortages were occurring somewhere between the shipper's facilities and Alpha's warehouses. In other words, the freight companies carrying the shipments had to be siphoning off portions of the shipments prior to arriving at Alpha. JJ also considered that Alpha's receiving personnel could very likely be involved in a conspiracy to defraud Alpha.

Before discussing his findings and conclusions or revealing his suspicions to anyone outside of Alpha's fraud team, JJ decided to conduct a number of additional tests, as most of his suspicions thus far were speculation. He could not be sure that receiving dock personnel were possible conspirators in fraud until he examined the copies of the receiving reports on partial shipments that had been forwarded to the accounting department. Logically, if the receiving dock personnel were conspirators, they would likely not notify the accounting department of the partial shipments. Otherwise, accounting would not approve a full payment to the shipper until the balance of the shipment was received. The only way to avoid this was to notify accounting that the full shipment had been received when in fact less than the full amount was actually received.

Proving it was easy for JJ. Using the partial shipment receiving reports he had selected from the warehouse files, he compared them to the copies that had been forwarded to accounting. He found the disparities he expected. Next he searched the inventory control records to determine whether the balance of the partial shipments had ever been received, to ensure the receiving dock personnel hadn't simply made errors by not indicating the partial shipments on the accounting copies. Finding none, JJ was now convinced that there was fraudulent activity occurring, and that the receiving dock personnel were most likely involved.

JJ met with the treasurer to disclose his findings. The treasurer agreed with JJ's initial findings and was somewhat relieved that the inventory shortage problem seemed to have been finally solved. He authorized an immediate criminal investigation, and a forensic accounting firm was engaged to confirm JJ's findings. The investigation revealed that a driver for the freight lines had conspired with three Alpha receiving dock employees to defraud Alpha by withholding a portion of selected shipments of goods being delivered. The diverted goods were then sold to various outlet stores and online. The driver and all three Alpha employees were arrested and successfully prosecuted.

Internal Controls

Implementing better controls and procedures could have prevented or detected the inventory shortage scheme that occurred at Alpha. Independent matching of documents is one measure that could have been used to identify their differences within the transactional documentation. In Alpha's case, the receiving section controlled the flow of packing slips and receiving documents to the warehouse and to accounting. Receiving was able to indicate on one set, for the warehouse, that only 900 were received, while indicating on the other set, for accounting, that 1,000 were received. There was no matching of the reports, and thus no means to detect a difference. A simple change in the flow of documents could ordinarily prevent or detect the theft of goods prior to the time the goods are received at Alpha's warehouses, as well as thefts by receiving employees after the items are received. After goods are received and counted, the paperwork should be properly marked for the items received by the receiving department and forwarded to the warehouse. A second copy should be forwarded to accounting, and once the warehouse completes their intake of the inventory, verifies the counts, and signs their forms, their copies of the receiving reports should be forwarded to accounting. Accounting should match and agree both copies of the receiving reports and packing lists. If less than the requested quantity of any item was received, both the warehouse personnel and the accounting department should be able to identify that fact.

Index

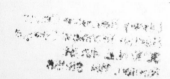